HEALTHCARE SPACES

No.1

Copyright © 2002 by Visual Reference Publications Inc.

Visual Reference Publications Inc.
302 Fifth Avenue
New York, NY 10001

Distributors to the trade in the United States and Canada
Watson-Guptill
1515 Broadway
New York, NY 10036

Distributors outside the United States and Canada
HarperCollins International
10 East 53rd Street
New York, NY 10022-5299

Library of Congress Cataloging in Publication Data:
Healthcare Spaces

Printed in Hong Kong
ISBN 1-58471-056-X

Book Design: Harish Patel Design Associates, New York

HEALTHCARE SPACES

No.1

ROGER YEE

Visual Reference Publications Inc., New York

CONTENTS

Introduction

Toiling amidst a hellish landscape in lower Manhattan that might have been portrayed by Hieronymus Bosch, doctors and nurses from some of New York's finest medical institutions did everything possible for injured survivors and exhausted rescuers of the World Trade Center catastrophe on September 11, 2001. They treated some patients on the spot using an extensive array of medical supplies and equipment rushed to the scene, while others with more serious conditions were taken to the city's hospitals. It was a dramatic demonstration that health care in the 21st century will draw upon institutions and facilities big and small to deliver services wherever they are needed. The traditional public image of the vast medical center located downtown in a major metropolis remains valid to this day, but it is increasingly being supplemented by smaller, nimbler neighborhood clinics, surgical centers, medical office buildings and other decentralized sources of health care that may provide the majority of services most patients will need.

Other signs of the powerful forces reshaping modern health care facilities can be seen within their walls. Health care administrators and planners, architects, engineers and interior designers are acknowledging that hospitals and other health care structures will never be finished if they are to remain responsive to the evolving needs of their service area populations. Not only must interiors be conceived as interchangeable spatial modules where functions will inevitably change, but the buildings that surround them are being prepared to accept additions and other modifications that will require ongoing internal adjustments.

The outcome of these changes is good news, nevertheless, for health care professionals, employers, insurers and the public. America's drive to contain health care costs is prompting hospitals to convert inpatient accommodations into outpatient facilities, reducing the time and cost of care by sending more patients home on the same day they receive treatment. Growing awareness of the power of a healing environment to enhance patient outcomes is guiding health care design towards a patient-centered focus that offers greater comfort, autonomy, dignity and support to patients, their families and friends. And the recognition that health care is about maintaining wellness in addition to treating illness is expanding the role of the health care institution within the community, inviting men, women and children to use its resources even in the absence of injury or disease.

Of course, evidence of these profound and life-affirming changes in the design of health care facilities is not yet visible in every city or town. But the newly completed, state-of-the-art hospitals, clinics and other health care environments documented in the following pages should help inspire decision makers in the private and public sectors as well as the public to undertake the effort. Health care facilities can never be the equivalents of hotels or homes, no matter how hard we try to de-institutionalize them. However, they can be designed to actively assist us in the often painful, disorienting and heroic task of recovering and maintaining our health.

Roger Yee
Editor

Anderson Mikos Architects ltd.

1420 Kensington Road
Oak Brook
Illinois 60523
630.573.5149
630.573.5176 (Fax)
dmikos@andersonmikos.com

Anderson Mikos Architects ltd.

Family Birthing Center
Mother and Baby Unit
Swedish Covenant Hospital
Chicago, Illinois

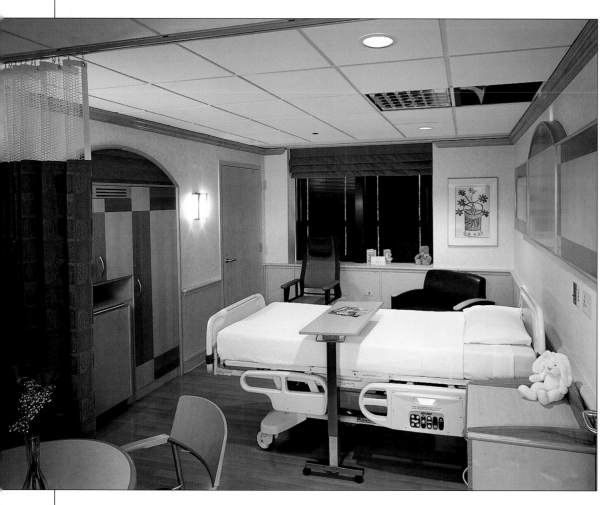

How do many OB/GYN patients differ from other patients? Pregnant women aren't ill. This basic fact has inspired the latest generation of women's health care facilities, including the new, 7,500-square foot Women's Health Center at Chicago's Swedish Covenant Hospital, designed by Anderson Mikos Architects ltd. The 12 single patient rooms and nursery in this post partum recovery unit do more than upgrade a 1914 building to current standards. They establish an upscale, comfortable and contemporary home-like atmosphere using such fresh design concepts as rich woods in the corridor, nurses station and patient rooms, patient rooms with Internet access and built-in TV armoires and refrigerators for family use, sophisticated lighting, and attractive contemporary furniture. Notes Saliba Kokaly, hospital director of construction and planning engineering, "The administration and nursing staff at Swedish are very happy with the results Anderson Mikos produced."

Opposite: Patient room.
Above: Nurses station.
Right: Nursery.
Photography: Mark Ballogg/Steinkamp and Ballogg Photographers.

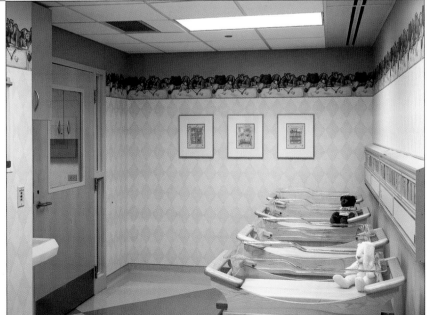

Anderson Mikos Architects ltd.

Central DuPage Health System
The Medical Offices of Stratford North
Bloomingdale, Illinois

Below left: Reception.
Bottom left:
Administrative station.
Opposite: Corridor.
Photography: Mark
Ballogg/Steinkamp and
Ballogg Photographers.

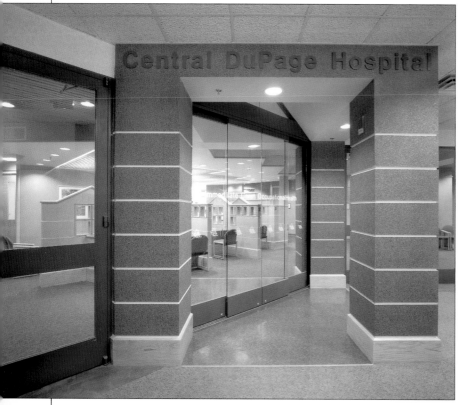

Finding your way in a health care facility can be difficult even in the best of circumstances. However, the challenge before Anderson Mikos Architects in designing the Medical Offices of Stratford North, part of the Central DuPage Health System in Bloomingdale, Illinois, was that the existing building chosen to house the 75,000-square foot facility had been a long vacant structure with a single, vast floor and no windows. To bestow a genuine sense of place to the new medical office building, which includes a 15,000-square foot immediate care facility, 2,500-square foot women's center and 2,500-square foot conference center as well as 55,000 square feet of medical offices, the architects have established clear, concise, skylit circulation patterns that have totally transformed the interior environment. These broad, sun-drenched corridors are easy for patients to follow, transmit natural light into each physician's suite, and provide memorable images that transcend the all-too-common institutional anonymity that prevails in health care facilities. The design then follows through by making the various destinations as accessible, self-explanatory and otherwise patient-friendly as possible, using floor plans that shift the building grid, creative configurations of drywall and millwork, a varied lighting design and comfortable and attractive furnishings to help patients get comfortable before they must say "ahh."

Medical Offices
at
Stratford North

Anderson Mikos Architects ltd.

Health Directions, Same Day Surgery
Chicago, Illinois

Advances in surgical technique and pressure to reduce cost by minimizing inpatient stays have nurtured stand-alone surgical centers where patient recovery takes from hours to an overnight stay. Such facilities are not only separate from hospitals, they can be conveniently located where people work or shop. A good example is the 14,500-square foot Same Day Surgery facility in Chicago, designed by Anderson Mikos Architects for Health Directions, which transforms a 1913 fashionable men's store on a downtown site into an award-winning environment with patient rooms, nursing facilities and administrative offices. Its warm, friendly ambiance is based on an innovative floor plan with all private patient rooms for pre- and post-procedure recovery that draws the patient into a rational flow from reception to dressing room, examination room and operating suite, all within a space that is flooded with natural light through high ceilings and glass block. The basic materials, including drywall, oak millwork and glass block, and a bright color scheme also help the facility achieve its distinctive appeal.

Above: Reception.
Below left: Corridor to patient rooms.
Below right: Operating suite.
Opposite: Private patient room.
Photography: Jay Wolke.

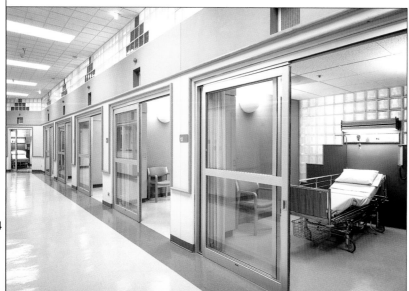

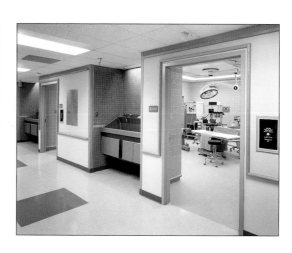

14

Anderson Mikos Architects ltd.

Children's Memorial Medical Center
Inpatient Unit Renovation
Chicago, Illinois

How can a hospital improve the outlook of sick children? In renovating the 85,000-square foot pediatric inpatient medical/surgical and intensive care nursing units at Children's Memorial Medical Center in Chicago, Anderson Mikos Architects identified two major design problems, namely incorporating decorative and wayfinding themes that were not too "childish" to appeal to all age groups, and creating space for parents and families within patient rooms and elsewhere. As a result, the six patient bed floors encompassing 96 inpatient beds, including a 30-bed NICU and a 28-bed PICU, feature multi-purpose rooms and patient play rooms, and offer provisions within all patient rooms for family activity, waiting, sleeping and Internet access, all enlivened by bold graphic patterns symbolizing "sky," "wind" and "forest." The design cannot promise to put smiles on young faces, but it has made the likelihood much greater.

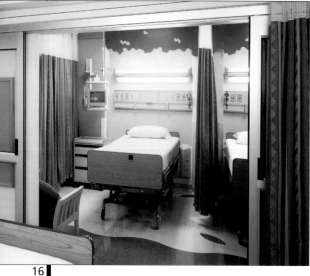

Above: *Nursing area.*
Far left: *Semi-private room.*
Left: *Patient play room.*
Photography: *Mark Ballogg/Steinkamp and Ballogg Photographers.*

Anshen+Allen, Architects

901 Market Street
San Francisco
California 94103
415.882.9500
415.882.9523 (Fax)

5055 Wilshire Boulevard
Los Angeles
California 90036
323.525.0500
323.525.0955 (Fax)

www.anshen.com
info@anshen.com

250 West Pratt Street
Suite 1000
Baltimore
Maryland 21201
410.528.7700
410.528.8456 (Fax)

88 Gray's Inn Road
London WCIXBAA
England, UK
011.44.207.663.2800
011.44.207.663.2801 (Fax)

Anshen+Allen, Architects

**New Main Hospital, Santa Clara
Valley Medical Center
San Jose, California**

If there is anything young Silicon Valley entrepreneurs share with impoverished Latino migrant workers in San Jose, California, it could be the desire for decent health care. In fact, a shining symbol of equal health care access is up and running on a 58-acre campus, namely the 346,000-square foot New Main Hospital for Santa Clara Valley Medical Center, designed by Anshen + Allen, Architects. The Center is the only hospital of 13 in the region to accept patients regardless of their ability to pay, and it nurtures them with floor plans that promote wayfinding, a stacking plan placing diagnostic and treatment on the lower floors and nursing units on the upper floors, and such welcoming facilities as a skylight-covered circulation spine, a cafe and gift shop anchoring opposite ends of the ground floor, and patient care floors that can easily convert from acute care to smaller intensive care units. You don't have to be rich or poor to appreciate care like this.

Above left: *Exterior.*
Above right: *Pediatric playroom.*
Right: *Acute care units.*
Opposite: *Lobby.*
Photography: *Richard Barnes (exterior, lobby), Robert Canfield (other interiors).*

Anshen+Allen, Architects

Kaiser San Francisco Medical Center
San Francisco, California

Kaiser Permanente constantly faces a deceptively simple yet infinitely challenging goal—to provide high-quality medical care at affordable cost. With this in mind, the HMO recently replaced, expanded and renovated an aging outpatient building in San Francisco to become the 260,000-square foot, eight-story Kaiser San Francisco Medical Center, designed by Anshen+Allen, Architects for 155 physicians serving 175,000 Bay Area members. The medical office building, part of a master plan for a projected 850,000-square foot campus of outpatient medical facilities, features ground floor retail, public street front courtyards and numerous "gathering halls." It's conceived as a comprehensive care clinic providing a full continuum of care in a "one-stop" site, where each clinic module serves up to 90 percent of the patient's medical needs. With offices and circulation on the perimeter and technologically intensive services at the core, it's also a "green" environment where daylight and natural ventilation help put San Franciscans at ease.

Above: *Exterior.*
Left: *Clinic module.*
Right: *Lobby.*
Opposite above: *Waiting room.*
Photography: *Mark Darley.*

Anshen+Allen, Architects

UC Davis/Mercy Cancer Center
Merced, California

As the first building of a larger replacement medical center to come, the 12,730-square foot, one-story UC Davis/Mercy Cancer Center, designed by Anshen+Allen, Architects, integrates its architecture, interior design and landscape to give patients a unique healing environment. A trellised, open-air entry court, dedicated garden for the infusion area and natural palette of finishes and furnishings link treatment with nature's cycles, so patients in the radiation oncology zone, medical oncology infusion area and outpatient clinics feel connected to everyday life. The Center sets an encouraging precedent for the future.

Above left: *Outpatient reception.*
Far left: *Infusion area garden.*
Left: *Entrance.*
Opposite: *Entry court.*
Photography: *Mark Luthringer.*

Anshen+Allen, Architects

UCSF Medical Center
Radiology Department
San Francisco, California

Left: Reception.
Above: Patient lockers.
Below: Imaging area.
Photography: Robert Canfield.

When the chairman of UCSF Medical Center's radiology department commented that since "we only do this once every 30 years, do it with quality, style and durability," everyone knew what he meant. The radiology clinic, part of a preeminent teaching hospital in San Francisco, was hindered by inefficient circulation flow, undersized spaces, lack of natural light and views and awkward spaces. With the recent remodeling of the 4,000-square foot facility by Anshen+Allen, Architects, these problems have been resolved, and the new setting is winning praised for its pleasurable work environment, complete with spectacular views of the Golden Gate Bridge.

Ballinger

One Commerce Square
2005 Market Street
Suite 1500
Philadelphia
Pennsylvania 19103.7088
215.665.0900
215.665.0980 (Fax)
www.ballinger-ae.com
contact@ballinger-ae.com

Ballinger

The Reading Hospital and Medical Center
Reading, Pennsylvania

Left: *Mill exterior.*
Below left: *Lunch room.*
Bottom: *Reception and public waiting.*
Opposite: *General office area.*
Photography: *Matt Wargo Photographer.*

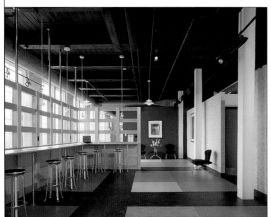

In a mill where silk was woven nearly a century ago, employees now operate the 7,000-square foot billing office of The Reading Hospital and Medical Center, Reading, Pennsylvania, designed by Ballinger. Although office space, the essence of the 1909 timber and masonry building still lingers. The new infrastructure, including mechanical, electrical, plumbing and fire safety systems, largely exposed to exploit 14-foot-high ceilings, complements existing windows and structural members. The original wood floors have been cleaned and refinished to contrast with the modular open-plan office furniture and colorful carpet patterns. The successful conversion of the mill has also depended on the development of an efficient and user-friendly workplace. Accordingly, the designers have introduced such appealing features as a "cranked" or angled corridor that guides visitors to the most direct path from the public waiting area to private offices and conference rooms. Exposed ducts and suspended light fixtures further define the "main street" circulation spine and ceiling plane, while dramatic colors enhance major building components, providing this old mill with a splendid new heart.

Georgetown University Medical Center
Department of Pediatrics
Washington, DC

Fitting a child's world within 500 square feet was the challenge Georgetown University Medical Center, Washington, DC, gave Ballinger. The hospital needed a "place of arrival" for the inpatient department, and the architects responded with the *Childlife Play Area* and *Adolescent Lounge.* Located directly across from the main access elevators, the play area stands just outside the inpatient care unit to welcome patients and visitors as a haven and destination. The themed space contrasts strongly with the hospital environment by introducing a richly varied setting that immediately stimulates children's interest. From the moment youngsters espy the *Station House,* a stop for the *Georgetown Choo-Choo,* they are happily drawn into a journey that leads them to the inpatient care unit. While the spatial elements are tightly knit, they acknowledge differences in patients' ages. Thus, the *Lounge* is stocked with computers, books and magazines, while the *Play Area* caters to more physical activities. It's hard to imagine adolescents ignoring such temptations as the *A2Z Forest,* home of the *Alphabet Grove,* whose trees bear letters.

Left: *Station House.*
Above: *View of adjoining corridors.*
Top: *Path to inpatient department.*
Photography: *Don Pearse Photographers.*

Hospital of the University of Pennsylvania
Philadelphia, Pennsylvania

No one ever wants to wake-up in an emergency room, but visitors will appreciate the new, 28,000-square foot emergency department (ED) of the Hospital of the University of Pennsylvania, designed by Ballinger and The Harrell Group. The new ED accommodates 60,000 acute and 20,000 urgent care patients using a completely paperless record—the first in the United States. Its environment raises the efficiency of care and enhances the comfort of patients with high technology and design innovations. The trauma area, for example, has permanent ceiling-mounted radiographic imaging, which displays digital images on computer stations throughout the unit, and a dedicated CT scanner. All patient care spaces, excluding trauma, are private rooms, featuring indirect lighting for glare reduction, and durable materials such as wood veneers and abundant glass, projecting a "friendly high-tech look" to transform a visit to this ED.

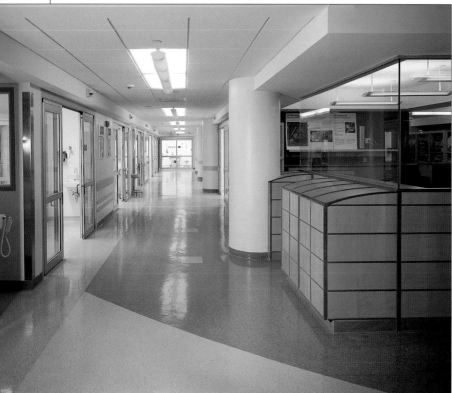

Above: *Waiting area.*
Left: *Acute patient care rooms and central nurses/ doctors station.*
Photography: *Matt Wargo Photographer.*

Ballinger

The Bryn Mawr Hospital
Jefferson Health System, Main Line Health
Bryn Mawr, Pennsylvania

Right: *Rotunda.*
Below: *Visitor lounge.*
Photography: *Matt Wargo Photographer.*

Ballinger has written a successful conclusion to the decade-long story of the 135,000-square foot West Wing addition to Bryn Mawr Hospital, Bryn Mawr, Pennsylvania, with the completion of the new main entrance and Warden Lobby. To avoid ramps, there are low, 13-foot floor-to-floor elevations that align with existing buildings; major mechanical feeds run vertically with minimal horizontal runs. The centralized registration and preadmission testing area is immediately behind registration booths to minimize walking distances. The entry offers appealing wayfinding features such as a rotunda at the crossroads of four circulation routes, a linear visitor lounge for maximum outdoor views, and distinctive, custom-designed indirect lighting fixtures for comforting, glare-free illumination, extending a gracious welcome to patients and visitors.

The Reading Hospital and Medical Center
Campus Redevelopment
Reading, Pennsylvania

Top: *The building forms a new courtyard around which the Visitor elevators, Cancer Center, and Heart Services are clustered. The Emergency Care entrance is a floor below.*

Above: *Main lobby and elevator bank to patient care.*
Top right: *Cancer Center entrance and lobby.*

A burgeoning community and the resulting demand for comprehensive clinical care have necessitated dramatic rethinking of The Reading Hospital and Medical Center's two million square foot/20-acre campus. Ballinger has designed a new seven-story, 340,000 square foot facility, which knits together disparate, fragmented programs and disjointed site circulation, while strengthening patient care in a warm, inviting atmosphere that provides the most advanced medical technologies. The brick and limestone structure melds with its neighbors, extending the campus' tradition of stately pavilions, airy connectors, and intimate courtyards. The three lower levels are devoted to Emergency Care, Cancer Services, and Heart Services, respectively. Each of these floors has a dedicated patient arrival portal and garage parking connected to a distinct lobby via conditioned walkways. The four upper floors house two wings of 32 beds or 21 ICU beds each. A prime motivation for the building's siting is its ability to greatly enhance patient's and visitor's overall experience and wayfinding while also maintaining staffing and operational efficiencies. An expanded, light filled visitor lobby with dedicated elevators affords access to the new nursing units as well as all existing inpatient beds. Its round tower is a memorable form that can be seen from afar and rediscovered from within. Elevator lobbies, like the Cancer and Cardiology waiting areas, overlook a contemplative courtyard. Parterre plantings and paving provide year round color, while in warm weather, a small fountain will add resonance.

BLM

161 Rock Hill Road
Bala Cynwyd
Pennsylvania 19004
610.667.8877
610.667.3940 (Fax)
www.theblmgroup.com
marketing@theblmgroup.com

BLM

Johns Hopkins at White Marsh
White Marsh, Maryland

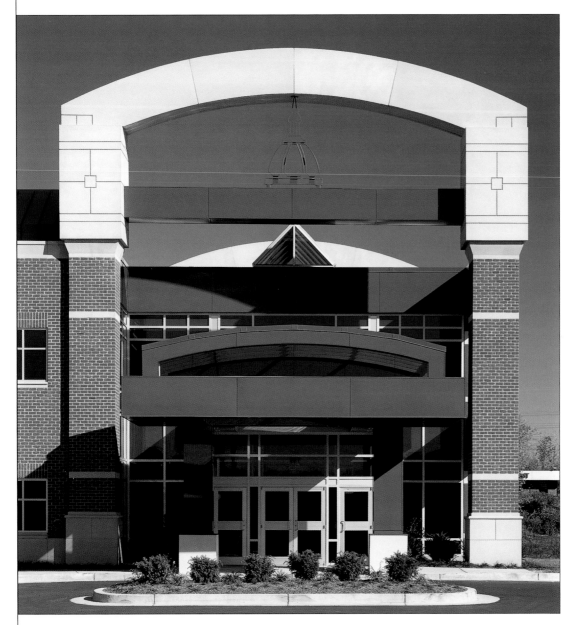

To serve growing populations in and around White Marsh, Maryland, Johns Hopkins Health System has developed a new, freestanding prototype health care facility, Johns Hopkins at White Marsh, designed by BLM. The architecture aids the success of the ambulatory care center by projecting the prestigious image of Johns Hopkins University, based on its historic Billings Building. In addition, the interior, including diagnostics on the first floor, visible from the atrium lobby, and primary and specialist physician group practices on the second floor, sharing a common reception/waiting area, are arranged for easy wayfinding. Who wouldn't welcome world-class medicine in a patient-friendly facility steps from home?

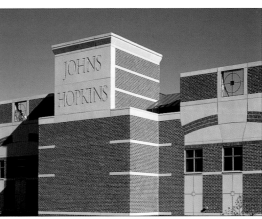

Above left: *Exterior at entrance.*
Far left: *Imaging center.*
Left: *Façade detail.*
Opposite: *Atrium lobby.*
Photography:
Jeff Totaro/Tom Crane Photography.

BLM

Hospitals will never be hotels or homes, but they can still learn much from these building types—particularly at their highly visible main entrances or "front doors." Thus, Christiana Care Health System's Patient Support Complex, Newark, Delaware, recently invited BLM to design an appropriate "front door" that would provide visual clarity for the entrance, 200 linear feet of weather-protected vehicular drop-off and pick-up, a "scale of entrance" appropriate for the size of the institution and volume of visitors, and accommodating waiting areas for the families of critically ill patients. One glance at the new, striking, 46,000-square foot main entrance, comprising a canopy/ visitor reception area, information center and family waiting, explains why it has elicited an "overwhelmingly positive" response from patients.

Above: View from lobby garden.
Right: Lobby and reception desk.
Opposite above left: Hospitality area.
Opposite above right: Railing detail.
Photography: Tom Crane/Tom Crane Photography.

BLM

Mercy Hospital Ambulatory Care Center
Wilkes Barre, Pennsylvania

Relocating ambulatory care from existing facilities in Mercy Hospital, Wilkes Barre, Pennsylvania, to a new, 65,000-square foot, two-story (plus parking), freestanding Ambulatory Care Center, designed by BLM, benefited the entire institution. For example, the Center made outpatient care more accessible than before, establishing a strong architectural context for wayfinding in a patient-friendly interior. Furthermore, Mercy's main entrance was reconfigured to differentiate outpatient and inpatient services, and the 100-year, flood-plain site featured ground level outpatient drop-off and parking, putting land use in harmony with local conditions. Everything has contributed to what Mercy calls the "crown jewel" of its facilities.

Left: Lobby.
Above right: *Reception desk.*
Top right: *Exterior.*
Photography:
Tom Crane/Tom Crane Photography.

BLM

Roxana Cannon Arsht Surgicenter
Christiana Care Health System
Wilmington, Delaware

Although the new, 38,000-square foot, one-story Roxana Cannon Arsht Surgicenter, Wilmington, Delaware, designed by BLM for Christiana Care Health System, is flanked by high-rise office buildings, it commands its site with strong massing, flexible floor plan and versatile structure. Why do patients give the Surgicenter the highest satisfaction ratings? Consider the one-way circulating loop that separates patient intake and discharge, fiber optic link to Wilmington Hospital for patient information, and healing environment featuring contemporary furnishings, indirect and natural light, and soothing color scheme.

Right: Lobby.
Below left: Prep and stage II recovery.
Below right: Exterior.
Photography: Jeff Totaro/Tom Crane Photography.

BLM

Somerset Medical Center
Patient Service Center
Somerville, New Jersey

Years of alterations can leave a hospital resembling a patchwork quilt. So when Somerset Medical Center, Somerville, New Jersey, developed a new, 21,000-square foot Patient Service Center, designed by BLM, it sought clarity through a new and highly visible main lobby incorporating such pre-admission services as reception, registration, outpatient laboratory and hospitality shop, and a new circulation spine connecting a new, 400-car visitor parking garage, the emergency department and the main public elevators to the patient wings. The new facility fills such an obvious need it's hard to imagine Somerset Medical Center without it.

Above: Lobby.
Upper right: Obstetrics unit.
Below: Exterior.
Photography:
Jeff Totaro/Tom Crane Photography

BSA Design

9365 Counselors Row
Suite 300
Indianapolis
Indiana 46240
317.819.7878
317.819.7288 (Fax)
www.bsadesign.com
info@bsadesign.com

BSA Design

Indiana University
Medical Campus
Indianapolis, Indiana

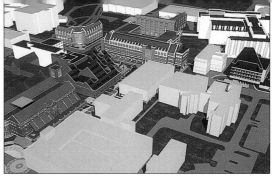

Above: *Overview, Indiana University Medical Campus.*
Far left, top: *Exterior, Cancer Research Institute.*
Far left, bottom: *Medical lab.*
Left: *Lobby/reception area.*

Far left: *J.W. Riley Hospital for Children, Phase III atrium (in association with Ellerbe Becket).*
Left: *Children's Cancer Center, overlooking courtyard.*

Far left: *Indiana Cancer Pavilion, atrium view to University Hospital.*
Left: *Entry courtyard with connection to University Hospital.*

BSA Design has proudly served Indiana University in planning and designing its Indianapolis medical campus for many years, developing the wide range of projects that are highlighted here. The 122,000-square foot Cancer Research Institute, for example, consolidates all cancer research programs at the Medical Center. The Phase III expansion of James Witcomb Riley Hospital for Children, 263,000 square feet of new construction and 16,000 square feet of renovation, upgrades the pediatric ICU, while the addition of the 23,700-square foot Children's Cancer Center introduces pediatric hematology/oncology and bone marrow transplant services. The Medical Science Center, 167,000 square feet of new construction and 22,000 square feet of renovation, enhances basic biomedical research and houses the labs of the State Department of Health. The 218,000-square foot Medical Research and Library Building joins two very dissimilar activities in one L-shaped facility. The 97,000-square foot Indiana Cancer Pavilion addresses the University's existing and future adult diagnostic and treatment programs and consolidates existing adult outpatient cancer clinics.

Above: Medical Science Center, south entry to Barnhill Plaza.
Above right: Atrium view

Right: Medical Research & Library Building, adjacent to Medical Science Center (in association with Ellerbe Becket).
Far right: Library interior (in association with Ellerbe Becket).

Right: Riley Outpatient Center (in association with KMD), overall camous view.
Far right: Exterior view.

BSA Design

Clarian Health Partners, Inc.
Cardiac Comprehensive Critical Care
Indianapolis, Indiana

What does it mean for BSA Design to create an unconventional, holistic healing environment at the 45,000-square foot, two-level Cardiac Comprehensive Critical Care unit in Methodist Hospital, Indianapolis, Indiana? For starters, provide patients everything they need within a three-zoned patient room. The staff zone cares for the patient with minimal disruption, the patient zone invites independence and a feeling of home, and the family zone provides personal storage, chair-bed, refrigerator, desk, telephone and Internet link. Says Joy L. Fay, the CCCC unit's director of clinical operations, "BSA Design turned our vision into a reality, and that's made a major difference to our patients and their families."

Above: Information desk.
Below left: Patient room.
Below right: Nurse's station.
Photography: Dan Francis/Mardan Photography.

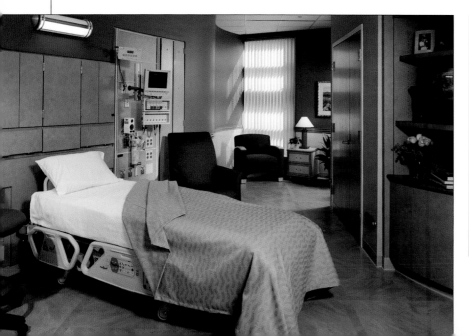

BSA Design

Memorial Medical Center
Koke Mill Medical Center
Springfield, Illinois

It's a vision that the Genius of the Prairie, Frank Lloyd Wright, would have appreciated. Memorial Health Systems and Orthopaedic Surgery Center of Illinois have jointly developed the 97,000-square foot Koke Mill Medical Center in Springfield to house the Center and offer advanced medical treatment in a new mammography center; outpatient physical, occupational and speech therapy and sports medicine facility; laboratory and radiology departments; and outpatient surgery and recovery. Not only has the advanced facility conceived by BSA Design been created swiftly and precisely, it honors Wright as architect of the Dana Thomas House, a Springfield landmark, with a design inspired by the master to lift the spirits of staff and patients.

Above: Main entry.
Right: Atrium.
Photography: Steve Pyle/Landmark Studios.

45

BSA Design

100 Navarre Place
South Bend, Indiana

Above: *Exterior looking southwest.*
Left: *West elevation.*
Below: *Main entrance and flying buttresses on north elevation.*
Photography: *Greg Murphey Studios.*

The recent completion of the 385,000-square foot, six-story 100 Navarre Place on the campus of Memorial Hospital and Health System, South Bend, Indiana, designed by BSA Design, does considerably more than create much needed space. The complex structure, comprising a three-story medical office building and ambulatory center atop a three-story parking garage for 600 vehicles, establishes strong links to its surroundings with a pedestrian bridge across the street to South Bend's primary hospital, an inviting main entrance and coffee shop/cyber cafe, The Medicine Cup, at street level, and handsome facades that acknowledge the campus's historic architecture. Better yet, patients leave their cars to enter a soaring atrium with campus views that welcomes them to comfortable, traditional interiors where the same civic spirit is flourishing.

46

BSA Design

Provena Covenant Medical Center Cancer Center Urbana, Illinois

Separate but equal might be a useful way to describe the Cancer Center at Provena Covenant Medical Center, Urbana, Illinois. Designed by BSA Design to establish a separate identity for the cancer care program while remaining part of the existing hospital, the 13,150-square foot, single-story structure includes clinical facilities, diagnostics, linear accelerator, simulator, mold/cast and support in a "spa-like" environment of arched roofs enclosing relaxed, curvilinear interiors that contrast markedly with the existing hospital building's crisp, orthogonal geometry. So while patients come for cancer treatment by a medical staff working with high-powered, state-of-the-art equipment, they can also enjoy the reassuringly open setting with generous windows, skylights, wood trim, resort-style furnishings and indoor plants—a healing environment for the 21st century.

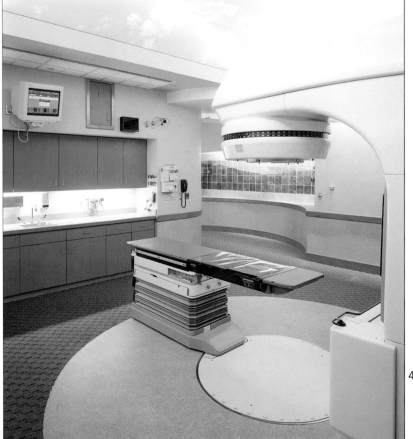

BSA Design

St. Vincent Hospital & Health Services
Seton Cove Spirituality Center
Indianapolis, Indiana

For over 100 years, St. Vincent Hospital & Health Services in Indianapolis has provided patients holistic care of the body, mind and spirit. Now, with the completion of the 14,000-square foot, two-story Seton Cove Spirituality Center, designed by BSA Design, St. Vincent is taking the same approach with its personnel and volunteers. Located on 30 wooded acres of the hospital's campus, the non-medical facility serves people seeking to develop and integrate spirituality into their daily lives. Among its great room and other formal meeting rooms, chapel, 20 guest bedrooms and kitchen/dining area, more than 10,000 staff members and guests have already come to experience a sense of peace and renewed spirituality.

Right: *Exterior.*
Below left: *Great room.*
Below right: *Chapel.*
Photography: *Henning Jobst Photography.*

48

Cannon Design

2170 Whitehaven Road
Grand Island
New York 14072
716.773.6800
716.773.5909 (Fax)
www.cannondesign.com
chilliers@cannondesign.com

Boston
Buffalo
Chicago
Jacksonville
Los Angeles
New York
St. Louis
Washington DC

Cannon Design

The Centers for Disease Control
Morgantown, West Virginia

Sharing a campus with West Virginia University Medical Center and ALOSH, an allied research agency, the 206,000 square foot, five-story NIOSH laboratory, an arm of the Centers for Disease Control, replaces outdated facilities with a world-caliber research environment. Prominently sited atop a hillside, the facility creates a new campus gateway, promoting scientific collaboration within the existing complex — aiding in the recruitment of talented investigators. A three-story skylit atrium creates a dynamic visual transition between the old and new facilities. The first floor is dedicated to administrative, reference library and educational facilities open to the University and public, while upper floors house specialized research programs. Laboratories line the perimeter of one wing of the L-shaped building and offices, the other, capturing natural light and outdoor views. Skybridge connections between facilities and common areas for study, training and conferences are consolidated at the union of the two wings.

Cannon Design

Mary Imogene Bassett Hospital Ambulatory Clinic
Cooperstown, New York

Left: *Exterior from river.*
Below: *Main lobby.*
Photography: *David Lamb Photography.*

Cooperstown is a national historic district, a community keenly attuned to the preservation of its character. In response, two stories of the 140,000 square foot, five-story ambulatory clinic are built into the hillside topography, while three stories are terraced above grade. A central common space serves as the building's principal focal point for patients, featuring views across the Susquehanna River to the surrounding countryside. Marble, natural wood, coffered ceilings, indirect lighting, and regional folk art and photography create an ambience more commonly associated with an elegant hotel. The center's many outpatient clinics use a modular design, emphasizing repetitive exam room and nursing station layouts for flexibility; also enabling clinics to expand into adjacent space to meet changes in service utilization and demand.

Cannon Design

Bretholtz Center for Patients and Families
Brigham and Women's Hospital
Boston, Massachusetts

The Center provides a supportive environment for patient admissions, family waiting, patient counseling and health education. In addition to serving as the primary point of patient interface, the Center serves the families of patients undergoing any type of prolonged procedure. Functioning as the hub of patient services, a reception desk in the main lobby offers electronic and voice communication with every department; high-tech kiosks in the Liaison Area display orientation programs; and the Kessler Learning Resource Center, a medical library, supports visitor research of post-procedural care and general health issues. Families of patients wait in a gallery-like setting curated by the Boston Museum of Fine Arts, to meet privately with physicians in any of seven consulting rooms.

Above: *Reception/Lobby.*
Right: *Kessler Learning Resource Center.*
Photography: *Richard Mandelkorn.*

Cannon Design

Curtis National Center for Treatment of the Hand and Upper Extremity
Baltimore, Maryland

Left: Overhead view of work station.
Far left: Main Patient Reception.
Below: View looking down Patient Service Corridor.
Right: Logistics points in hand therapy area house equipment and specialized hand splinting supplies.
Photography: Michael Dersin Photography.

Named for hand surgery pioneer, Dr. Raymond Curtis, the renovated, 27,000 square foot, two-story Center at Union Memorial Hospital, meets virtually all patient needs through effective facility planning in five critical areas: Patient Care, Network Research, Information, Technology and Training — accommodating the multiple functions of clinic, rehabilitation, work hardening; and as part of its national charter, library/archival, teleconferencing and administrative spaces. Workstations are organized in a circular pattern, using a combination of custom casework and portable tables that appear as groupings of inviting tables and chairs. Working in the center of the circle with patients seated around the perimeter, allow therapists the flexibility to concentrate on a single patient or supervise multiple patients. This configuration creates an atmosphere of camaraderie, a radical departure from the traditional clinical environment — not only improving service and patient morale, but also lessening the duration of patient visits. "This project discards the cold, scary and impersonal image of most medical facilities by placing the therapeutic stations in a serene and beautiful open setting," noted the AIA.

Cannon Design

Whitby Mental Health Centre
Whitby, Ontario, Canada

A model for new psychiatric facilities well into the 21st century, the design of the 500,500 square foot Whitby Mental Health Centre, a joint venture of Crang & Boake/Cannon Design/ Moffat Kinoshita, is the most comprehensive project of its kind undertaken in Canada in 25 years. The 325-bed replacement hospital features diagnostic, therapy and outpatient areas; education center with lecture hall and classrooms; recreation center with gym and pool; dining hall, coffee shop; administration and support services. The park-like setting of the former hospital reflected the therapeutic benefits of access to nature and the residential quality of free standing patient cottages. Retaining these positive characteristics, yet condensing operations into a single structure, the two-story facility is comprised of seven in-patient and six diagnostic and treatment support buildings. A 1,500 foot long enclosed corridor, "the Street," seams them together so that the entire hospital functions as a linear village.

Left: *Dining area.*
Lower left: *Courtyard.*
Lower right: *Main Lobby.*
Photography: *David Whittaker Photography, Patrick Kennedy Photography.*

Earl Swensson Associates, Inc.

2100 West End Avenue
Suite 1200
Nashville
Tennessee 37203
615.329.9445
615.329.0046 (Fax)
www.esarch.com
info@esarch.com

Earl Swensson Associates, Inc.

Baptist Memorial Hospital–Collierville
Collierville, Tennessee

Collierville, Tennessee is the site of the new, 287,384-square-foot Baptist Memorial Hospital-Collierville, designed by Earl Swensson Associates, Inc., as well as a formerly rural town with a proud past. Charged with giving the community a hospital and an integrated physicians' office building that would honor its heritage, the design team has organized the facility like a town square with a main circulation path that bisects the various components and promotes wayfinding. Accordingly, the hospital's programmatic requirements are clustered around the central court, letting all departments be represented by symbolic or figurative storefronts that are complemented by such distinctive public spaces as the gift shop, wellness center, information resource center, dining room, chapel and waiting areas. The facility's considerable volume is broken down by an architecture of brick and slate that deftly evokes the town's gazebo, clock tower, church and train station. Gratified by Collierville's response, Rick Lassiter, the hospital's assistant administrator, reports, "We constantly hear such comments as 'I feel like I'm at home here.'"

Left: *Patient room.*
Below: *Nurses station.*
Below left: *Dining room.*
Bottom: *Exterior.*
Opposite: *Central court.*
Photography: *Jonathan Hillyer.*

Earl Swensson Associates, Inc.

Samaritan North Health Center Phase II
Dayton, Ohio

Left: Rehabilitation and sports medicine center. **Below:** Exterior. **Opposite:** Lobby. **Photography:** Craig Dugan/Hedrich Blessing, Gordon Morioka.

Patients, families and friends entering Samaritan North Health Center, Dayton, Ohio, don't need to know that the complex has been enlarged with the completion of the 155,713-square-foot Phase II addition and 247,660-square-foot parking deck, designed by Earl Swensson Associates, Inc. The seamless expansion provides new accommodations for an outpatient surgery center, well-being center, second linear vault for the cancer care center and additions to existing areas for physical therapy, cardiac rehabilitation and occupational therapy. Consequently, the two structures are perceived as one with four sides, each having its own entrance in an elevation of brick and arches. The transformation continues indoor, with a pedestrian mall joining the new, sky-lighted and barrel vaulted lobby with the existing one, producing the largest freestanding outpatient facility in America. "Earl Swensson's triumph at Samaritan North Health Center is evidenced by such patient comments as, 'The moment I walk into this place I feel cared for,'" observes Anne L. McNeill, FACHE, vice president operations for Good Samaritan Hospital.

Earl Swensson Associates, Inc. Mayo Clinic Hospital
Phoenix, Arizona

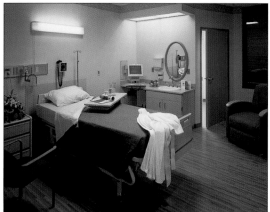

Determined to be Phoenix's premier health care institution, the Mayo Clinic Hospital asked Earl Swensson Associates, Inc. to design a physical plant worthy of a branch of Minnesota's famed Mayo Clinic. That objective is clearly visible in the 440,000-square-foot, 176-bed, acute care medical/surgical hospital, which incorporates an interstitial floor for added MPE and communications capacity when the hospital expands. Its state-of-the-art, patient-friendly environment includes a 14-room surgical suite for inpatient and outpatient surgery, intensive care/critical care unit, short-stay recovery unit for outpatient surgery, sleep studies lab, general medical/surgical rooms, transplant facility, numerous other departmental accommodations, dining, gift shop, chapel and public conference areas, all organized around an energy-conserving five-story atrium. Dr. Michael B. O'Sullivan, chair, board of governors of the Mayo Clinic Scottsdale, proudly notes that the National Research Corporation has declared Mayo "number one" in terms of "best nurses, best doctors, hospital image and reputation" in Phoenix.

Upper left: *Outdoor dining.*
Upper right: *Patient room.*
Top right: *Exterior.*
Right: *Intensive care unit.*
Opposite: *Atrium.*
Photography: *Mark Boisclair.*

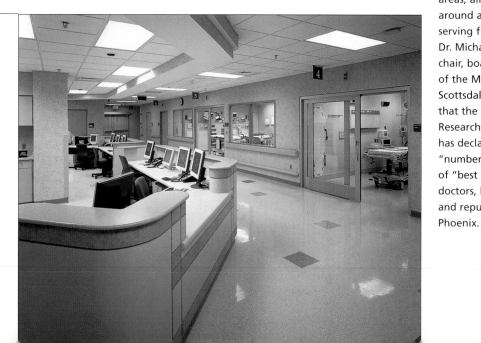

Angel and Paul Harvey Atrium

Earl Swensson Associates, Inc.

Fayette Community Hospital
Fayetteville, Georgia

Right: Exterior.
Below: Reception.
Photography:
Jonathan Hillyer.

How can a health care institution assure incoming patients they will receive a positive, emotionally supportive and therapeutically beneficial experience? Fayette Community Hospital's 141,000-square-foot, 100-bed hospital and 80,000-square-foot medical office building, designed by Earl Swensson Associates, Inc., establishes an attractive environment with strong wayfinding that begins with a hotel-like main entrance for most patients—emergency being separate—where clear signage and a soothing fountain lead to the reception desk, lounge seating and various medical facilities. Tracey L. Coker, Fayette's executive coordinator, support services, comments, "It is functional, logically arranged, and beautiful."

FKP Architects, Inc.

8 Greenway Plaza
Suite 300
Houston
Texas 77046
713.621.2100
713.621.2178
www.fkp.com

FKP Architects, Inc.

Visitors entering the new, 215,000-square foot Health and Wellness Center at Christus St. Catherine, Katy, Texas, may find the experience more like a trip to a shopping mall then visiting a hospital. Indeed, the Center, designed by FKP Architects as the first phase of a 67-acre master planned development called Christus Park, branches off a 700-foot long, gently curving Mall that serves as the circulation spine. The design gives the public easy access to the Center's health care services, which include two medical office buildings, registration, birthing center, surgical facilities, emergency room and imaging center. Taking cues from retail design, the Center welcomes its visitors to large, spacious interiors bathed in natural light from two central courtyards with public elevators located between them. And what else could complete the design but an inviting Food Court that spills out into the Mall?

Right: Landscaped courtyard.
Below left: LDRP room.
Bottom: Two-story mall.
Opposite: Mall exterior.

FKP Architects, Inc.

Christus St. Joseph
The Pavilion - Ambulatory Care Center
Houston, Texas

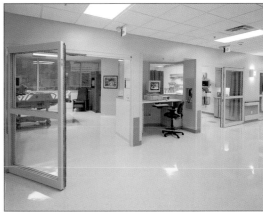

America's continuing shift from inpatient care to ambulatory services is having a profound impact on individual health care institutions. Christus St. Joseph, Houston, Texas, had a desire to create a convenient outpatient facility with clear wayfinding to function as the "front door" of the institution. The result was the recent completion of The Pavilion - Ambulatory Care Center, a 215,000-square foot, five-level facility, and its 175,000-square foot parking garage, both designed by FKP Architects. The wayfinding for the outpatients begins in the parking garage with its connected bridges that lead directly to the new ambulatory care center as well as the other existing buildings. The Pavilion was then designed with a 4-story atrium focused upon the 2-story chapel. All waiting areas for the building occupants—out patient registration, pre-admission testing, diagnostic imaging, surgery and intensive care are located directly off that atrium for visibility and accessibility. The view from each waiting area is directed towards the chapel to provide spiritual comfort and enhance the healing environment.

Aboveleft: *Outpatient main entrance.*
Above right: *ICU.*
Left: *Atrium mezzanine.*
Opposite: *Chapel.*
Photography:
Aker/Zvonkovic Photography.

FKP Architects, Inc.

**Northeast Medical Center Hospital
Southwest Tower
Humble, Texas**

Aboveleft: LDRP room in Southwest Tower.
Above right: Elevator lobby in Professional Office Building.

Below: Exterior of Northeast Regional Cancer Center.
Opposite: Public waiting and registration at Northeast Regional Cancer Center.
Photography: Aker/Zvonkovic Photography.

Like the patients they treat, hospitals need regular examinations to assess their health. For example, an ongoing review of Northeast Medical Center Hospital, Humble, Texas, by FKP Architects uncovered a range of renovation and new construction projects needed by the 237-bed institution. Among the most significant results of this effort is the 165,000-square foot Southwest Tower addition, a replacement building for existing major diagnostic and patient care services on the campus. The recently completed structure houses an eight-OR surgical suite, post-anesthesia care unit, central sterile processing, women's LDRP birthing center, intensive care and acute care inpatient beds, administrative and support services, set within a warm and inviting environment featuring hospitality-style furnishings, indirect and accent lighting, and good circulation for wayfinding. With improving reruitment and referral of physicians, plus rising utilization by growing numbers of area residents, the new Tower is proving to be the right prescription.

FKP Architects, Inc.

Presbyterian Hospital of Plano
Plano, Texas

Left: *Main lobby.*
Below left: *Cafeteria.*
Below right: *New entrance exterior.*
Photography: *Michael Ralph, Aker/Zvonkovic Photography.*

In an act that speaks volumes about the evolving relationships among health care professionals, patients and families, Presbyterian Hospital of Plano, Plano, Texas, had one main requirement for FKP Architects in updating its existing 100-bed facility: Create a state-of-the-art health care facility that doesn't feel like a hospital. The recently finished 160,000-square foot renovation, 160,000-square foot expansion, 95,000-square foot new medical office building and 95,000-square foot, 600-car, new parking structure herald a rebirth for the Hospital in time for an influx of outpatients. The impact of patient-focused care is unmistakable. Expanded and new facilities for OB/GYN, orthopedics, ER, surgery, cardiopulmonary and more occupy spacious, sun-lit interiors appointed in wood, stone, comfortable furniture, accent lighting and warm colors, redefining the word "hospital."

Hellmuth, Obata + Kassabaum, P.C.

Atlanta
Berlin
Chicago
Dallas
Greenville
Hong Kong
Houston
Kansas City
London
Los Angeles

Mexico City
New York
Orlando
San Francisco
Shanghai
St. Louis
Tampa
Tokyo
Warsaw
Washington DC

Hellmuth, Obata + Kassabaum, P.C.

The Lied Transplant Center
University of Nebraska Health System
Omaha, Nebraska

Since transplant patients must remain hospitalized for up to several months with their care partners, the University of Nebraska Health System elected to create a fresh vision of the health care environment for the new, 220,000-square foot, 11-story Lied Transplant Center in Omaha, designed by Hellmuth, Obata & Kassabaum. The facility, which includes a cancer clinic, 88 "cooperative care" patient suites, research laboratory, information center and parking, consolidates pre- and post-transplant services in a setting that exploits the effects of psychoneuroimmunology by providing a non-institutional design to promote healing. Among the features yielding such benefits are patient suites with the comfort, convenience and appearance of hotel accommodations, a spatial setting for wayfinding that establishes a strong hierarchy of spaces ranging from an atrium whose cof-fered and illuminated ceiling depicts star constellations to elevator lobbies and corridors, and healthy common areas characterized by natural light and glare-free cove lighting, natural materials, works of art, indoor plantings and an outdoor garden. Even feng shui concepts have been followed that patients need not know about to appreciate.

Above right: Reception.
Right: Outdoor garden.
Below: Patient suite.
Opposite: Atrium.
Photography: Paul Brokering.

Hellmuth, Obata + Kassabaum, P.C.

New York Presbyterian Hospital
New York, New York

Below: Nurses station.
Opposite top: Exterior on New York's East River.
Photography: Maxwell Mackenzie (exteriors), Walter Dufresne (interiors).

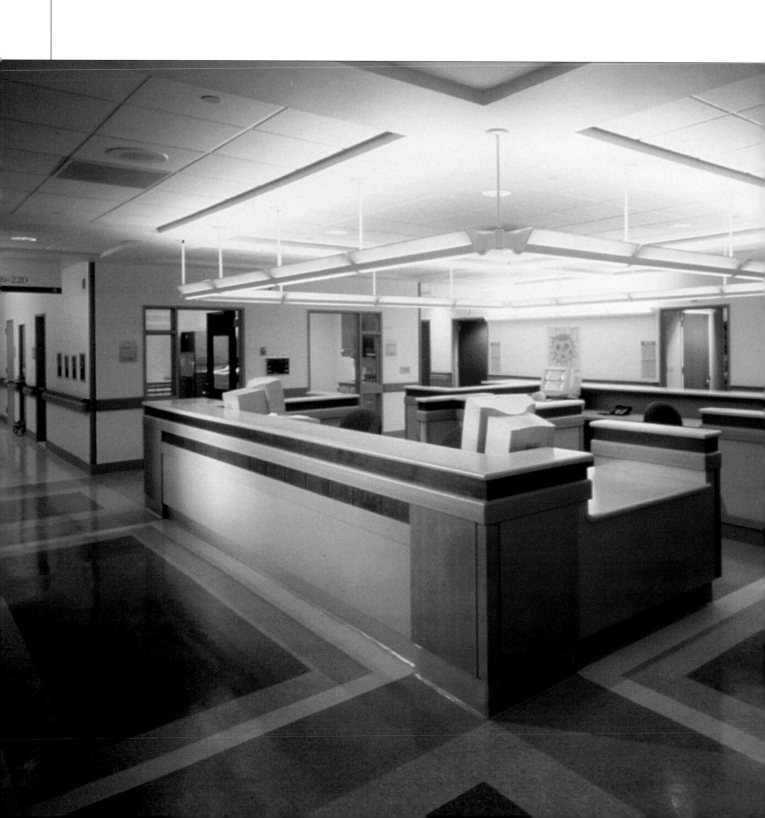

Health care facilities age unpredictably, with changing medical technologies and evolving health care delivery systems rendering some obsolete while reprieving others. A case in point is New York Presbyterian Hospital, on Manhattan's Upper East Side, an innovative hybrid of existing and new construction designed by Hellmuth, Obata & Kassabaum with Taylor Clark Architects. As a 50-year-old, three-block, two million-square-foot-plus building, New York Hospital/Cornell Medical Center was no longer adequate to house its 1,048 inpatient beds. A comprehensive assessment of its suitability determined that all nursing units and high-technology diagnostics would be best served by new construction, while other groups could be accommodated in remodeled space. Accordingly, a new, 854,000-square foot addition was built on the eastern edge of the campus to house impatient diagnostic and treatment departments, a new emergency department, a new operating suite of 19 operating rooms, and a new labor and delivery suite. With 970 beds, including 760 in the new facility, New York Presbyterian has been splendidly rejuvenated.

Hellmuth, Obata + Kassabaum, P.C.

Northwestern Memorial Hospital
Chicago, Illinois

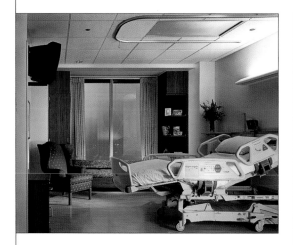

Left: View from patient room.
Upper left: Private patient room.
Upper right: Nurses s tation
Opposite: Main lobby.
Photography: Scott McDonald & Justin Maconochie/Hedrich Blessing.

The Windy City residents who depend on Northwestern Memorial Hospital for 80,000 out-patient visits and 26,000 admissions a year inspired Northeastern University to mandate that "patients are first" in developing its new, two million-square foot, 26-story, 492-bed replacement hospital and ambulatory care center, designed by Hellmuth, Obata & Kassabaum. The sizable structure incorpo-rates ambulatory care, private patients' rooms, cancer center, cardiology, diagnostic imaging, emergency, ICU, pedi-atrics, surgery, adminis-tration and parking. Yet its patient-focused envi-ronment of wood accents, fine fabrics, comfortable furniture, indirect lighting, panoramic views, excel-lent wayfinding and Internet access in all rooms assures that each patient feels special here.

Hellmuth, Obata + Kassabaum, P.C.

Ontario Cancer Institute
Princess Margaret Hospital
Toronto, Ontario, Canada

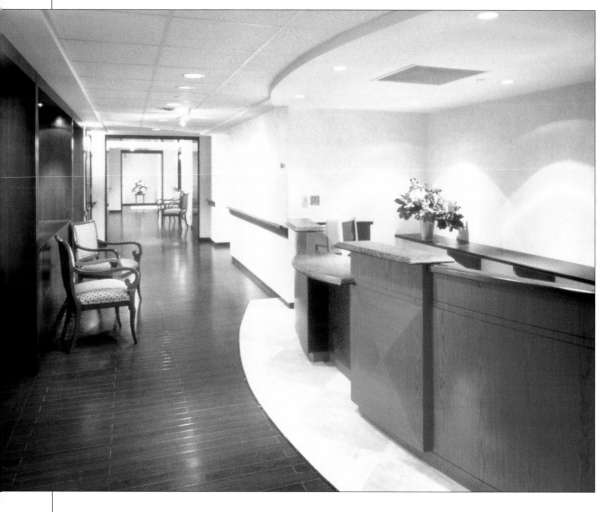

Merging and consolidating the Toronto Hospital and Ontario Cancer Institute/Princess Margaret Hospital Centers of Excellence required more than a 146,700-square foot, six-floor renovation by Hellmuth, Obata & Kassabaum. Four key objectives defined the creation of Canada's largest cancer clinic: developing a new facility to expand the patient base by responding to market-driven issues, implementing the project on a fast-track basis, maintaining interrupted operations, and providing a setting to keep attracting talent in cancer treatment and research. In response, the design provides each of 10 clinic sites with its own entry, reception, waiting and resource library areas as well as examination and treatment areas, and appoints them in wood, natural and warm tones, glass, architectural lighting and non-institutional furnishings. Add such special spaces for patients and families as library/resource rooms, juice bar and meditation room, and what emerges is an exceptional, holistic institution for Canada.

Above: Clinic site reception.
Far left: Juice bar.
Left Public meeting area.
Photography: Design Archive.

Helman Hurley Charvat Peacock Architects, Inc.

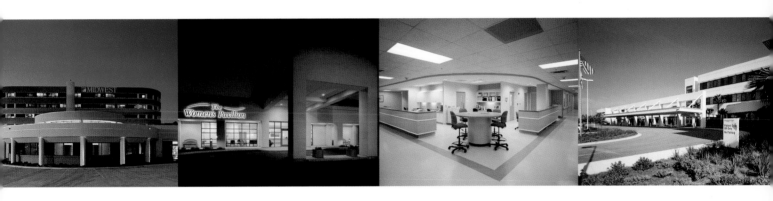

1053 Maitland Center Commons Blvd.
Suite 101
Maitland
Florida 32751
407.875.2722
407.475.0811 (Fax)
www.hhcp.com
hfd@hhcp.com

Helman Hurley Charvat Peacock Architects, Inc.

Midwest Regional Medical Center Emergency Department Midwest City, Oklahoma

Anyone who has spent time in an emergency room awaiting treatment for minor injuries or illnesses would appreciate having the average wait reduced by 71 percent. Yet that's just one reason why the new addition to the Emergency Department at Midwest Regional Medical Center, in Midwest City, Oklahoma, designed by Helman Hurley Charvat Peacock Architects, can effective-ly handle over 66,000 visits annually, the high-est volume ED in Oklahoma. The creation of separate trauma, emergent and fast-track pods as well as a com-prehensive breast center to the existing structure supports a new "nurse-first" triage system, whereby an immediate assessment and assign-ment to an appropriate level of care is made as the patient arrives. The 33 new examination bays and other special features such as minor surgery capability, an OB emergency station for emergency deliveries and bedside registration reveal why Dr. Dan Donnell, Midwest Regional's medical direc-tor of emergency medi-cine, can proudly say, "We have planned this emergency facility to be like no other."

Helman Hurley Charvat Peacock
Architects, Inc.

Riverview Regional Medical Center
The Women's Pavilion
Gadsden, Alabama

Right: Main lobby and waiting area.
Below left: Exterior.
Below right: Typical LDRP suite.
Photography: Ramond Martinot.

Addressing women's health care needs is the driving force behind such facilities as the new, 12,784-square foot Women's Pavilion at Riverview Regional Medical Center, Gadsden, Alabama, designed by Helman Hurley Charvat Peacock Architects. The Pavilion, which comprises eight LDRP suites, one C-section room, a two bed recovery room, a two bed observation room and various support spaces, establishes an elegant and peaceful environment for patients through careful planning, good circulation and sensitive interior design. Its exterior acknowledges the existing, multi-story hospital which it expands by maintaining the older structure's color scheme and paneling pattern. Inside, the LDRPs are characterized by high ceilings with soffits and embossed tile, wood flooring, molding, comfortable furniture, framed mirrors and pendant lighting, details that reappear elsewhere, as well as space for dining and a sleeper love seat. Finding the right balance for women between a home-like setting and a state-of-the-art infant security and health care environment is a worthwhile goal reflected successfully at the new Women's Pavilion.

Helman Hurley Charvat Peacock Architects, Inc.

Carolina Pines Regional Medical Center
Hartsville, South Carolina

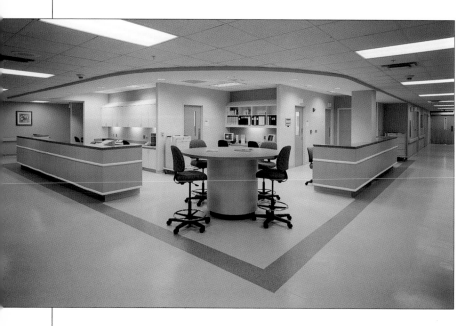

Patient-friendly health care facilities are reaching out to the communities they serve as the health care industry becomes market driven, the public exercises the power of choice, and everyone benefits from healing environments. Consider the new, 175,000-square foot, 116-bed Carolina Pines Regional Medical Center, in Hartsville, South Carolina, designed by Helman Hurley Charvat Peacock Architects. All patient rooms are private, equipped with bathroom, telephone, television and space for family and friends. In addition, Carolina Pines offers a 13-bay emergency department for "nurse-first" triage, a 12-bed ICU, seven-room surgery suite configured for a changing mix of inpa-

tient/outpatient procedures, state-of-the-art imaging department, dedicated women's center, pediatric wing, expanded outpatient services, 55,000-square foot medical office building, and such amenities as an attractive entrance area with gift shop and chapel, inviting cafeteria and comfortable family and visitor waiting area. A "main street" spine corridor organizes everything, aids wayfinding and assures the community that this hospital exists to care for and comfort them.

Above: Nurses station.
Right: Main entrance.
Opposite: Family and visitor waiting area and spine corridor.
Photography: Ramond Martinot.

Helman Hurley Charvat Peacock Architects, Inc.

Heart of Florida Regional Medical Center
Haines City, Florida

To emphasize outpatient care and emergency services, the new, 120,000-square foot, 75-bed Heart of Florida Regional Medical Center, in Haines City, Florida, is designed by Helman Hurley Charvat Peacock Architects for convenience and easy access to services—with good consequences for fast growing Central Florida. Patient flow and turnaround time for emergency and ambulatory care, for example, have been improved by co-locating clinical diagnostic and treatment services. Registration/information serving inpatient, outpatient and emergency is immediately inside the entry area, reducing the number of FTEs required. Inpatient rooms are all private, have views of the landscaped campus and accommodate families, friends and overnight stays. Currently being expanded to raise its bed count and enlarge its emergency department, the Center is proving its value to the community in numerous ways.

Above: Patient drop-off area.
Right: Curtain wall with brise-soleil.
Photography: Everett & Soulé.

88

Hillier

500 Alexander Park CN 23
Princeton
New Jersey 08543
609.452.8888
609.452.8332 (Fax)

www.hillier.com

New York
Newark
Philadelphia
Washington
Scranton
Kansas City
Dallas
London

Hillier

Seabrook Village
Tinton Falls, New Jersey

Today's retirees are more active than ever, and a new senior living facility that exemplifies the possibilities is 132-acre Seabrook Village, in Tinton Falls, New Jersey, designed by Hillier. Working in harmony with the surrounding community and wetland environment, Seabrook operates three "neighborhoods," self-contained clusters of residential buildings served by their own community buildings. The opportunities for activities extend indoors and outdoors. As residents enjoy the comfort of their 445 independent, assisted or skilled-care living units, they can explore the grounds that complement the 504,684-square foot, Victorian-style seashore architectural complex, or take part in a wide range of social, civic and educational events at their community buildings and other facilities—including some that are shared with Tinton Falls—expanding the horizons of modern senior living.

Top: *Exterior with natatorium.*
Above: *Indoor swimming pool.*
Opposite: *Neighborhood porte-cochere.*
Photography: *James D'Addio.*

Hillier

The Bristol-Myers Squibb
Children's Hospital at
Robert Wood Johnson
University Hospital
New Brunswick, New Jersey

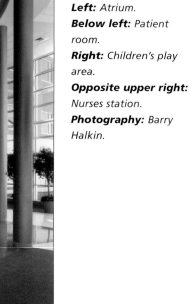

Above: *Exterior.*
Left: *Atrium.*
Below left: *Patient room.*
Right: *Children's play area.*
Opposite upper right: *Nurses station.*
Photography: *Barry Halkin.*

An exciting, interactive environment is one of the happy discoveries for children entering the new, 146,000-square-foot Bristol-Myers Squibb Children's Hospital at the prestigious Robert Wood Johnson University Hospital in New Brunswick, New Jersey, designed by Hillier. The institution provides state-of-the-art diagnostic and treatment servic-es, 62 inpatient beds and same-day surgery in a setting created to deal with children's physical and emotional needs. Besides offering such special features as a technologically advanced family education and resource center, the hospital gives children and families spacious patient rooms where parents can stay overnight, circulation paths for easy wayfinding and advanced medical facilities set in sunny, inviting spaces. Of course, what distinguishes the interiors in children's eyes are such delights as sculptured gardens, a starlit atrium, gift shop and exploration paths, which reduce stress and make return visits seem like adventures.

Mountainside Hospital
Montclair, New Jersey

Although patients of 400-bed Mountainside Hospital, in Montclair, New Jersey, have been increasingly directed to extensive outpatient services rather than extended stays in acute care, everyone has used one entrance—until now. The new, 24,000-square-foot expansion and 30,000-square-foot remodeling by Hillier changes everything, starting with a generous canopy over a new outpatient drop-off area that ushers outpatients into a spacious, three-story lobby leading to clinical services on three levels as well as an existing MRI facility.

Combining new construction and renovation enhances outpatient services substantially. The ground level, for example, offers patients and staff such spaces as an outpatient registration and testing area, patient resource library, center for women's health and physical therapy area. Going above, the first floor comprises an imaging department with a special procedures suite and same-day surgery service, while the second floor (third level) houses additional outpatient physicians' office suites and a connector walkway to the existing second floor.

Above: Exterior.
Right: Main lobby.
Opposite: Outpatient registration.
Photography: James D'Addio.

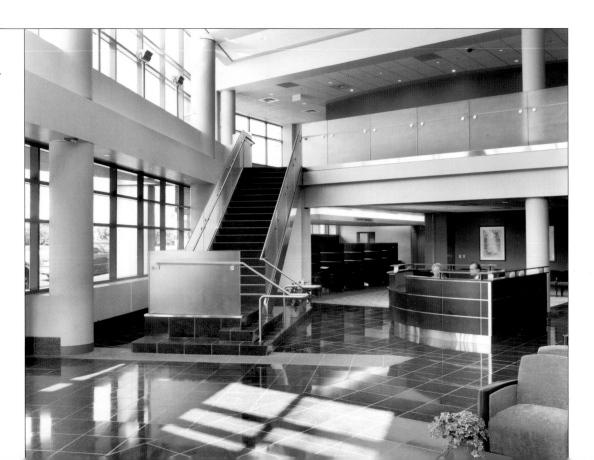

Trexlertown Wellness Center
Lehigh Valley Hospital & Health Network
Trexlertown, Pennsylvania

Convenient, one-stop, health-care "shopping"—in a former department store? That's where you'll find Lehigh Valley Hospital & Health Network's handsome, new Trexlertown Wellness Center, in Trexlertown, Pennsylvania, anchoring a mall. To facilitate the 30,000-square foot conversion, Hillier examined the patient experience and staff activities to identify needs, develop meaningful spaces and create a patient-friendly environment for family practice, women's health, diagnostic services, community health, education and wellness, plus suites leased to physicians. Can you enter from the mall? Of course.

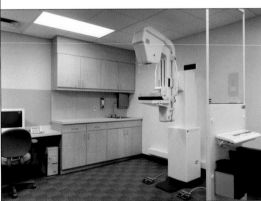

Top: *Reception desk.*
Above: *Mammography.*
Right: *Waiting area.*
Photography: *Barry Halkin.*

HKS Inc.

1919 McKinney Avenue
Dallas
Texas 75201.1753
214.969.5599
214.969.3397 (Fax)
www.hskinc.com

HKS Inc.

Valley Children's Medical Center
Madera, California

To call Valley Children's Medical Center in Madera, California, a 618,000-square foot, three-story, 214-bed hospital scarcely begins to describe this special place. From the colorful, village-like exterior to the playful, earthy interior, the facility designed by HKS Inc., promotes healing by giving children a mentally stimulating environment designed around the theme, "Our Universe." The theme is developed in clinic spaces as "Our World," patient areas as "Our Solar System," and ancillary locations as "Our Environment," using media ranging from paint to fiber optics to produce a state-of-the-art setting where physicians and other health care professionals treat children who know it's meant just for them.

Above: Roof and façade detailing.
Left: Patient waiting area.
Right: Patient room.
Opposite: Dining.
Photography: Kelly Petersen (interiors); Khaled Alkotob (exterior).

HKS Inc.

Health Central
Ocoee, Florida

Right: Exterior.
Below left: Waiting area off atrium lobby.
Below right: Patient room.
Opposite: Atrium lobby.
Photography: Michael Lowry.

One-stop shopping may not be how many consumers envision their health care, but residents of Ocoee, Florida in metropolitan Orlando are praising the concept at Health Central, a new, 275,000-square foot replacement hospital designed by HKS Inc. The institution makes health care easy to obtain by combining a 141-bed, six-level acute-care hospital with 50,000 square feet of office space for physicians, health services and related retailing. Each of the center's components—ambulatory care, inpatient care and education—is grouped around a central, organizing atrium, and physicians' offices and hospital facilities are intermingled on each floor so physicians can directly monitor their patients' progress. The innovative space plan is complemented by advanced medical technology supported by computers, a "mobile technology port," an airport-like docking zone where new diagnostic and treatment devices can be trucked and connected as needed, and a physi- cal environment that is attractive, light-filled and as non-institutional as possible. One-stop shopping for health care looks like a smart buy here.

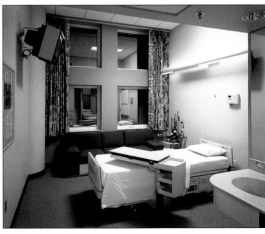

HKS Inc.

Utah Valley Regional Medical Center
Women's and Children's Addition
Provo, Utah

Since giving birth is now a family affair, the new, 225,000 square foot Women's and Children's Addition to Utah Valley Regional Center, designed by HKS Inc., provides delivery rooms to accommodate multiple family members. This is one of many details acknowledging user input at the facility, which includes a labor and delivery unit, mother/baby unit, nurseries, neo-natal intensive care unit, pediatric intensive care unit and women's and children's outpatient services. The healing architectural environment is complement-ed by the latest technology, concerned staff, and family and friends. Amenities include soothing interiors with expansive daylighting, comfortable waiting areas for family and friends, and pediatric intensive care rooms with overnight accommodations for the parents to spend the night. It's easy to see why expectant mothers from other communities are flocking here

Below: North elevation.
Bottom: Patient room.
Right: Main lobby.
Photography:
Ed LaCasse.

102

Baptist Health Ambulatory Care Center
Little Rock, Arkansas

Above left: *Atrium.*
Above right: *Exterior.*
Photography: *Ed LaCasse (interior); Wes Thompson (exterior).*

Directing patients to a new "front door" for outpatient services is critical for the new, 129,000-square foot Baptist Health Ambulatory Care Center, designed by HKS Inc. The southern portion of the Baptist Health Systems' campus is being reorganized for more ambulatory care, with the new Center offering radiation therapy, breast center, heart institute, office space, patient/family waiting pavilion and general physician lease space. The Center's significance as a "front door" will become more evident as a planned concourse guides patients from the ambulatory care entry into a series of outpatient centers or pavilions to be added as the campus grows. Meanwhile, patients entering the Center's atrium will find waiting areas organized around the perimeter, corridors that separate public, staff and patient circulation, and a friendly environment like an open "front door."

Klett Organization

112 York Road
Jenkintown
Pennsylvania 19046
215.576.1580
215.884.2195 (Fax)
arch@klett-arch.com

Klett Organization

Chandler Hall
Newtown, Pennsylvania

How do you provide a "home-like" environment for 96 assisted living residents? Chandler Hall, a 25-year-old senior care Quaker facility in Newtown, Pennsylvania, recently retained the Klett Organization to design a handsome, new, 119,000-square foot residential complex of four "manor houses" on two adjacent sites, with each pair of manor houses adjoining a community building. Visiting a manor house is like entering a private residence, as you proceed through the living room, library and parlor to the dining room, the doorway to the community building. Each community building shelters unique functions shared by all residents. Bedroom wings, by contrast, are secluded from community activities. Whether residents take part in small family visits and group gatherings or large social or religious events, they'll feel at home in Chandler Hall.

Above: Exterior of Manor House.
Below left: Exterior of community building.
Below right: Detail of exterior fascia.
Photography: JDN Photography.

Left: Dining room.
Below left: Living room.
Below right: County kitchen and activity room.

Klett Organization

Crozer Keystone Medical Office Building
Springfield Township, Pennsylvania

Medical office buildings play a vital role in attracting physicians and patients to health care systems, as can be seen in the new, 60,000-square foot, three-level Crozer Keystone Medical Office Building in Springfield Township, Pennsylvania, designed by the Klett Organization.

The facility, which encloses corporate headquarters for the Crozer Keystone Healthplex as well as medical offices for individual physicians, takes its place beside two existing structures, a medical office building and a hospital. Its design consequently addresses significant exterior and interior needs. On the outside, the architecture introduces a 600-foot long connecting bridge that establishes a physical connection among the medical office buildings, the hospital and the Healthplex, and site grading makes room for two levels of covered parking and easy access for patients and physicians. Indoors, medical offices are tailored to suit individual physicians' needs, while common areas project Crozer Keystone's institutional identity, reinforcing its ties to the community.

Left: Exterior.
Above: Boardroom.
Opposite: Entrance lobby.
Photography: JDN Photography.

William G. Rohrer Center for HealthFitness
Voorhees, New Jersey

Above left: *Exterior.*
Above right: *Entry lobby.*
Opposite: *Natatorium.*
Photography: *JDN Photography.*

The emerging importance of wellness in contemporary life reflects a growing realization among health care professionals, business leaders and the public that promoting long-term physical fitness and healthy living is far more life-sustaining and cost-effective than intervening during acute episodes of preventable diseases. This holistic view of well-being, which benefits from being presented in a life-promoting physical environment that appeals to patients, is effectively demonstrated in the attractive, new, 83,000-square foot, two-story William G. Rohrer Center for HealthFitness in Voorhees, New Jersey, designed by the Klett Organization. As a state-of-the-art facility, encompassing a gymnasium, aerobics, natatorium with lap pool, exercise pool and warm water therapy pool, men's and women's spas, locker facilities, administration, conference center, delicatessen/dining area, and child care facility—all attached to a medical office building offering a cardiologist, cardio rehab, pain management and other related specialties—the Center is designed and constructed for heavy, continuous use at all hours of the day by young and old,

veterans and novices alike. Its distinctive materials, including an exposed, heavy timber wood frame structure, concrete roof tile, brick masonry veneer exterior, precast coping, precast lintels, glass block and curtain wall system, ensure that getting fit and staying well have never looked better.

Above: *Gymnasium.*
Right: *Locker facilities.*
Far right: *Child care.*
Below right: *Aerobics.*

Langdon Wilson
Architecture Planning Interiors

1055 Wilshire Boulevard
Suite 1500
Los Angeles
California 90017
213.250.1186
213.482.4654 (Fax)
asadkhan@earthlink.net
bsmith@langdonwilson.com

www.langdonwilson.com

18800 Von Karman Avenue
Suite 200
Irvine
California 92612
949.833.9193
949.833.3098 (Fax)
pallen@lw-oc.com

455 North Third Street
Suite 333
Phoenix
Arizona 85004
602.252.2555
602.252.2760 (Fax)
mschroeder@lwphx.com

Langdon Wilson
Architecture Planning Interiors

Cedars-Sinai Medical Center
North Critical Care Tower
Los Angeles, California

Above: Main elevation.
Left: Aerial view with helipad.
Below left: Elevation facing main hospital.
Opposite: Connecting bridges to main hospital.
Photography: Eric Koyama.

Because the historic Brown-Schuman Building at Cedars-Sinai Medical Center in Los Angeles was severely damaged by the 1994 Northridge earthquake, Langdon Wilson has designed the new, 230,000-square foot, eight-story, 180-bed North Critical Care Tower to align with the existing hospital floor by floor. The North Critical Care Tower will be more than a replacement facility, however, when it's com-pleted. Besides providing state-of-the-art intensive care units with comput-erized monitoring of patient rooms, medical/surgical unit, acute rehabilitation unit, and other critical care facilities, all joined by connecting bridges to the main hospital's oper-ating rooms, it will accommodate an 18-bed expansion of the Emergency Department, an enlargement of the Cedars-Sinai Cancer Center, and a rooftop helipad. The Tower's architecture may even reshape the character of its West Los Angeles intersection, introducing a dynamic massing of metal curtain walls accented by cantilevered glass-enclosed floor lob-bies facing the Hollywood hills.

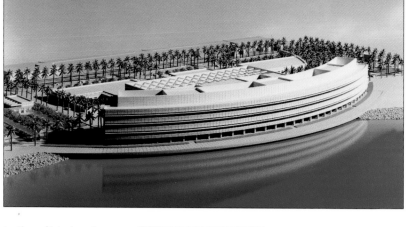

Langdon Wilson
Architecture Planning Interiors

Chest Diseases Hospital
Kuwait City, Kuwait

How should Islamic principles and traditions, environmental conditions in the Persian Gulf and sophisticated health care facility design be combined to serve the people of Kuwait? The Chest Diseases Hospital, a 500,000-square foot, 320-bed institution in Kuwait City, Kuwait, designed by Langdon Wilson for the Ministry of Health in Kuwait and currently under construction, provides an inspiring example. The hospital will be highly functional, technologically advanced, flexible for expansion and other modification, and sensitive to staff and patients —without losing sight of energy and water conservation in a region where fresh water is as prized as petroleum. Internally, the administrative, clinical and patient room functions are grouped to achieve an efficient operation and exploit expansive views of the Gulf. On the outside, the graceful forms of the component buildings include such special features as a curving structure along the Gulf and contemplative "oasis gardens" accessible to patients, visitors and staff members.

Above: *View from the water.*
Below: *Aerial view of site.*
Photography: *Mark Lohman.*

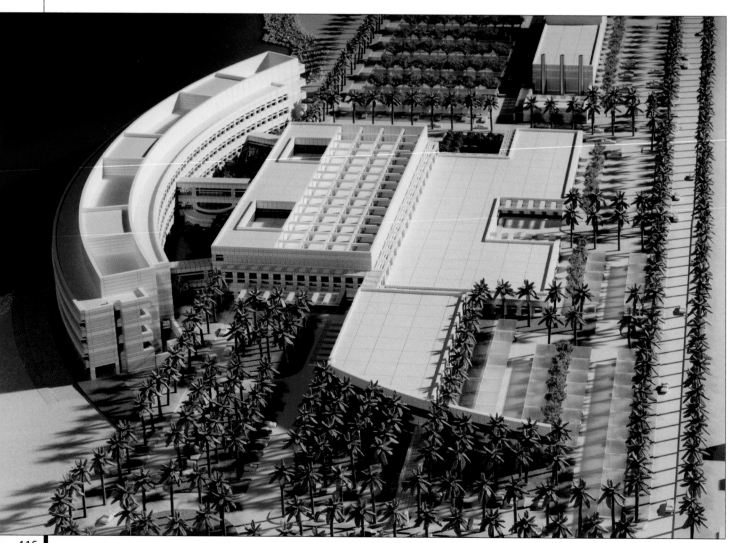

Langdon Wilson
Architecture Planning Interiors

Ahmadi Hospital
Ahmadi, Kuwait

Right: Rendering.
Below right: Aerial view of model.
Photography: Eric Koyama.
Illustration: Robert Kaminsky.

Winner of an international architectural design competition, the 580,000-square foot, 300-bed Ahmadi Hospital in Ahmadi, Kuwait, designed by Langdon Wilson, is a striking facility that maximizes the potential for future expansion based on a relatively compact footprint while minimalizing corridor lengths and exploiting outside views for all patient rooms. A typical patient care unit is conceived as a triangle with patient rooms lining the exterior walls, the nurses station at the center of the triangle and patient corridors that are 50 percent shorter than those in conventional floor plans. The versatile design will have no difficulty expanding 33 percent to 400 beds.

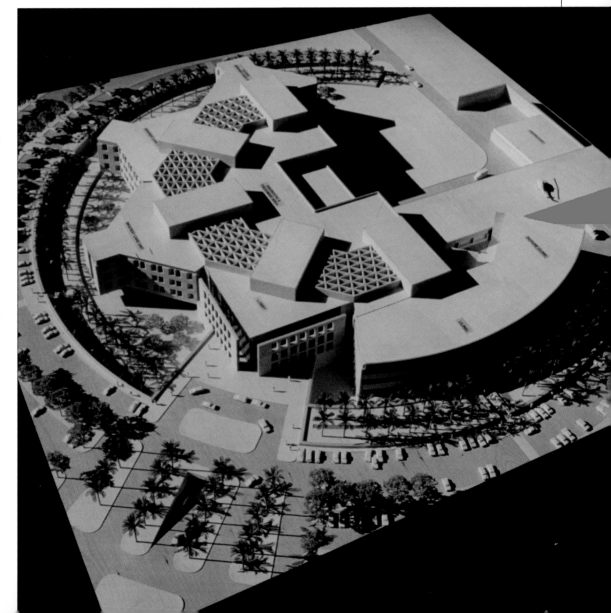

Langdon Wilson
Architecture Planning Interiors

Kaiser Riverside Medical Center
Riverside, California

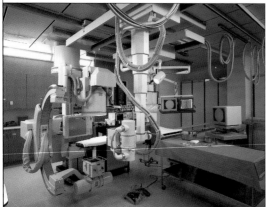

A young, growing population in Riverside, California provided the incentive for the rapid development of the 504,000-square foot Kaiser Riverside Medical Center, designed by Langdon Wilson, encompassing an acute care hospital, clinic annex and medical office building. Since the complex was based on a prototype created by Langdon Wilson for Kaiser Woodland Hills, actual construction work commenced with uncommon speed. From the owner's authorization, planning, design, contract docu-

mentation and OSHPD approval to the start of construction took just under eight months. The clinic annex was the Center's most critically needed facility, so it was completed a full year before the acute care hospital was ready for occupancy. Yet the accelerated schedule should not obscure the fact that the Center's overall health care environment has been carefully conceived to be patient-oriented, with an easily comprehended circulation plan for good wayfinding, restful interiors intended to wel-

come patients and streamline the daily routine of staff, and attractive furnishings specified for comfort and durability. That's good health care design at any speed.

Top: *Exterior.*
Above: *Operating room.*
Right: *Main lobby.*
Photography: *Milroy & McAleer.*

Langdon Wilson
Architecture Planning Interiors

Martin Luther King Jr./Charles Drew Medical Center
Trauma Care and Diagnostic Imaging Center
Los Angeles, California

Having overtaken Chicago as America's second most populous city years ago, Los Angeles is challenged to meet the health care needs of an expanding school age population, and an encouraging barometer of progress is the new Martin Luther King Jr./Charles Drew Medical Center, designed by Langdon Wilson. The 180,000-square foot facility, which comprises pediatric acute care, child care center, trauma care, diagnostic imaging center and ambulatory care services, was developed in consecutive phases—starting with a replacement facility for pediatric acute care and child care center, and concluding with a new trauma care and diagnostic imaging center. Though the facility circulates acutely ill children,

trauma patients and others with serious conditions very efficiently, it also offers a healing environment of color coordinated spaces, back-lit glass block walls, coffered ceilings and handsome furnishings that welcome all patients—and draw praise from professionals like Larry Colvin, director, Health Facilities Planning Services for Los Angeles County, who commended Langdon Wilson for "your designs and your staff's ability to listen and translate our needs into a functional program and a successful design."

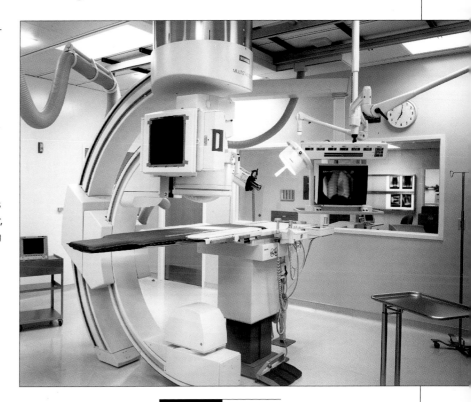

Above: *Imaging unit.*
Below left: *Trauma care.*
**Below right: Exterior.*
Photography: *Milroy & McAleer.*

119

Langdon Wilson
Architecture Planning Interiors

Greater Bakersfield Memorial Hospital
Bakersfield, California

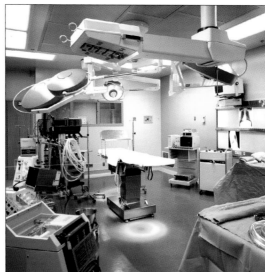

Bakersfield, California, may never be a tourist attraction, but its oil fields play a vital role in the Golden State's economy nonetheless. So it was appropriate when Greater Bakersfield Memorial Hospital, a non-profit, community acute care institution, asked Langdon Wilson to develop a three-phase master plan for the expansion and updating of the existing 206-bed facility. Phase I saw the construction of a new, 147,000-square foot, 144-bed (including ICU/CCU) patient tower and a bridge connecting the new and existing buildings, the enlargement of the central plant, and the remodeling of the existing labor/delivery area. Phase II began with the expansion of maternity facilities and will conclude with the building of a second patient tower. A reassuring sign of the plan's success is that the hospital's operations continue uninterrupted as its future unfolds.

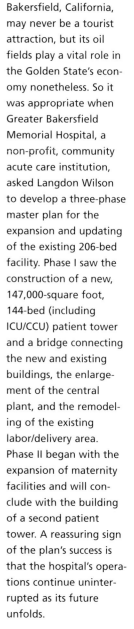

Above left: Nurses station.
Above right: Operating room.
Left: Exterior.
Photography: Milroy & McAleer.

Larsen Shein Ginsberg + Magnusson LLP Architects

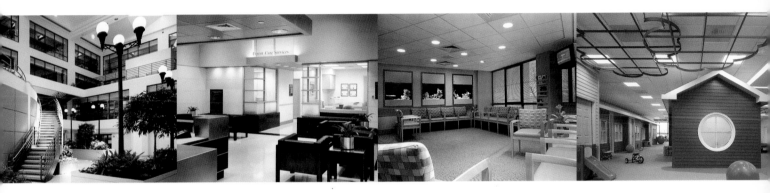

170 Varick Street
New York
New York 10013
212.803.0300
212.803.0370 (fax)
www.lsgmarchitects.com
email@lsgmarchitects.com

Larsen Shein Ginsberg + Magnusson LLP Architects

Phillips Ambulatory Care Center
Beth Israel Medical Center
New York, New York

Above left: *Corridor.*
Above right:
Conference center.
Right: *Waiting room.*
Opposite: *Atrium with conference center.*
Photography: *Elliott Kaufman, Barry Halkin.*

While caring for all patients is a universal goal of health care institutions, providing health care services to all payer classes with a single, high standard of care in a single, well-designed setting distinguishes Manhattan's 300,000-square foot Phillips Ambulatory Care Center, designed by Larsen Shein Ginsberg + Magnusson. Consequently, the facility, which includes suites for primary care, adult medicine, pediatrics, ENT, OB/GYN, neurology, opthalmology, speech and hearing, and urology, has creatively transformed an existing, four-story atrium and its surrounding floors into a bright, airy, patient-friendly environment. Notes Denise Pelle, the Center's vice president for administration, "This facility allowed us to quickly meet our goal to see over a thousand patients a day in intimate and appropriate settings and without undue waiting time. Patients are satisfied, so are doctors, and our practices are growing beyond expectation."

Larsen Shein Ginsberg + Magnusson LLP Architects

University Health Services Center
New York University
New York, New York

Left: Urgent care unit.
Lower left: Physical therapy.
Bottom: Waiting area.
Opposite: Entrance to urgent care services.
Photography: Barry Halkin.

For insight into the medical services required to support a student population of over 25,000, including the largest percentage of international students of any American university, just follow an NYU student to the new 58,000 square foot University Health Services Center at the edge of the Manhattan campus. The Center, designed by Larsen Shein Ginsberg + Magnusson, mitigates the tedium and anxiety patients typically feel during a diagnostic visit by creating a pro-active environment where students can turn to a variety of educational programs as well as primary care, urgent care, women's health, allergy and immunology, gener-al immunization, HIV testing and counseling, optometry, and physical and occupational therapies. Created in a loft-like space carved from a former manufacturing building, the interior projects an efficient, comfortable and appealing modern design. "The architectural look and feel of the place rivals that of any medical facility in the city," says Ernesto Ferran, Jr., MD, the Center's executive director.

Urgent Care Services

**Larsen Shein Ginsberg +
Magnusson LLP Architects**

Long Island Jewish Medical Center
Ambulatory Chemotherapy Transfusion Unit
New Hyde Park, New York

Chemotherapy infusion is inherently stressful and anxiety-provoking. Not surprisingly, Long Island Jewish Medical Center, New Hyde Park, New York, decided to mitigate the negative effects of the regimen through its new, 22,000-square foot Ambulatory Chemotherapy Transfusion Unit, designed by Larsen Shein Ginsberg + Magnusson. To achieve this goal, the architects looked beyond the basic functional program for the treatment modules, nurse/work areas, satellite pharmacy, exam, treatment and other ancillary functions—as well as the prevailing design stereotypes. Their solution establishes the 20-station unit as an oasis of assurance, spaciousness and a careful balance between privacy and community, using such design elements as continuous glazing of the exterior wall, a gracefully arched wood ceiling, handsome wood cabinetry that functions as space dividers between treatment cubicles, and a subtle light-

ing scheme that casts an indirect glow over the entire space. "Both patients and staff have reacted to the unit with joy, enthusiasm and appreciation," indicates the director of the unit. In fact, the Medical Center has identified the unit as a prototype for all future renovation projects.

Above: Support facilities.
Left: Treatment cubicles.
Upper right: Reception.
Right: Waiting room.
Photography: Andrea Brizzi.

Larsen Shein Ginsberg + Magnusson LLP Architects

Blythedale Children's Hospital
New Occupational & Physical Therapy Department
Valhalla, New York

What could coax smiles from children who are being treated for birth defects, developmental delay or the effects of catastrophic accidents? The 5,500-square foot New Occupational & Physical Therapy Department in Blythedale Children's Hospital, Valhalla, New York, designed by Larsen Shein Ginsberg + Magnusson, does this by inviting the children into a world where the therapy facilities are enriched by images, forms and colors that are fun and stimulating. Watching the youngsters, who may come in wheelchairs or on stretchers for inpatient or outpatient services, as they enter their own, individual treatment spaces, can even make adults smile. These facilities are part of a village of colorful little houses standing apart from an open space for exercise mats, tricycles and other therapeutic play.

Above: View from department entrance.
Right: Entrance to individual treatment space.
Photography: Andrea Brizzi.

Lee, Burkhart, Liu, Inc.

2890 Colorado Avenue
Santa Monica
California 90404
310.829.2249
310.829.1736 (Fax)
www.lblarch.com

Lee, Burkhart, Liu, Inc.

Lemoore Naval Air Station Replacement Hospital and Ambulatory Care Expansion Lemoore, California

Above: *Exterior at night.*
Top: *Main lobby and circulation spine in atrium.*
Opposite: *Atrium clerestory.*
Photography: *Erhard Pfeiffer Photographers.*

Meeting the military's health care needs—with an emphasis on preventative medicine and obstetrics—was the goal of the Naval Facilities Engineering Command in developing the new, two-story, 155,000-square foot Replacement Hospital and Ambulatory Care Expansion for Lemoore Naval Air Station, Lemoore, California, designed by Lee, Burkhart, Liu. The facility typifies the projects entrusted to the firm during 15 years of developing over 15 million square feet of health care, research and educational space. Equipped with 16 inpatient beds and extensive clinical and ambulatory services, it exemplifies the modular "universal room" concept with treatment rooms, exam rooms, support rooms and convertible outpatient clinics designed for quick and economical reprogramming. Noted R.E. Elster, Officer in Charge, Naval Healthcare Support Office, "The professional performance and total cooperation of the entire LBL team and its engineering disciplines are particularly to be commended."

Lee, Burkhart, Liu, Inc.

Department of Veterans Affairs Ambulatory Care Center
Sepulveda, California

Right: Exterior at main entrance.
Below: Sun-filled interior.
Photography: Tom Bonner Photography.

Major earthquake damage to an existing inpatient facility cleared the way for the new, 245,000-square foot Department of Veterans Affairs Ambulatory Care Center in Sepulveda, California, designed by Lee, Burkhart, Liu in association with SMP. Yet the new Center is also a model for the entire V.A. system, offering a complete range of outpatient diagnostic and treatment services in an innovative "bedless" hospital. On a campus comprising new telecommunications and central plant facilities, seven renovated buildings plus the new ambulatory care building, the Center consolidates most patient services into a single, patient-friendly location supporting primary ambulatory care and education (PACE) clinics, specialty clinics and ancil-

lary services. Each of four PACE clinics offers the patient diverse medical specialties in a single environment, and each patient remains with one clinic permanently. Based on their success here, PACE clinics are spreading to other V.A. medical centers nationwide.

Lee, Burkhart, Liu, Inc.

LAC+USC Medical Center Replacement Project
Los Angeles, California

Left: Light-filled stair tower.
Right: Main entrance to Outpatient Center.
Below: Site plan.
Photography: Adrian Velicescu.

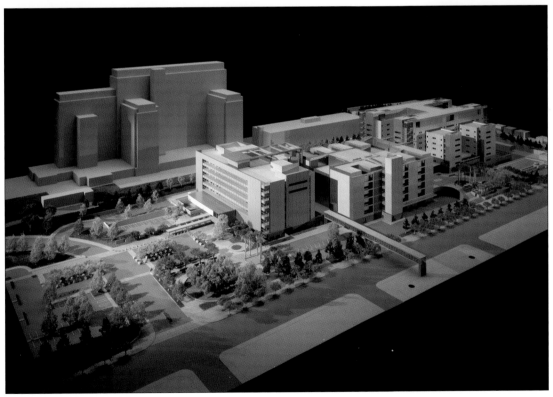

A structure like the LAC (Los Angeles County) + USC (University of Southern California) Medical Center Replacement Project, a 1,475,000-square foot structure under construction in Los Angeles, designed by Lee, Burkhart, Liu in association with HOK, illustrates the needs of America's largest public teaching hospital. Encompassing a 600-bed inpatient facility, ambulatory care, diagnostic services, trauma services and regional tertiary care, children's day care center and central plant, the new Center serves the diverse needs of medical students, multi-cultural patient population, and progressive delivery systems—and looks ahead with a flexible design anticipating an incremental 80-bed patient tower for the County of Los Angeles.

Lee, Burkhart, Liu, Inc.

Childrens Hospital Los Angeles
Marion and John E. Anderson Building
Los Angeles, California

America's surging population of schoolage children has inspired a new generation of children's hospitals combining the latest medical technology and sophisticated design strategies to create healing environments for children. An impressive example of the new approach is the Marion and John E. Anderson Building for Childrens Hospital Los Angeles, designed by Lee, Burkhart, Liu. This three-story, 105,000-square foot facility introduces a surgery center with 14 state-of-the-art surgery rooms and attendant recovery area along with a main entry, lobby and grand pedestrian concourse, and reflects the understanding that when children are hospi-

talized, entire families become involved and should be accommodated. Consequently, strong links have been made to families and the community by integrating into the general scheme such child-responsive elements as abundant daylight and views of hospital gardens through numerous windows and skylights, clear wayfinding via the concourse and other dramatic interior spaces, vibrant colors, eye-catching themes and multi-cultural iconography expressed in graphics and freestanding forms, attractive furnishings, engaging interactive exhibits, a gift shop and a McDonald's restaurant. The design's cumulative impact has been quickly noticed. Commenting on

a recent open house and reception, John H. Welborne, Director of the Foundation for Childrens Hospital Los Angeles, said, "Guests have told us how they were so impressed by the variety and quality of the exhibits, building design and displays they saw."

Above: *Entry foyer.*
Right: *Exterior at main entry.*
Opposite: *Children's reading area with fanciful furnishings.*
Photography: *Erhard Pfeiffer Photographers.*

Above: *Admitting area.*
Right: *A donor wall display along the concourse.*

Loebl Schlossman & Hackl

130 East Randolph Drive
Suite 3400
Chicago
Illinois 60601.6313
312.565.1800
312.565.5912 (Fax)
design@lshchicago.com
www.lshdesign.com

Loebl Schlossman & Hackl

Loebl Schlossman & Hackl

Resurrection Medical Center
Chicago, Illinois

Like epic stories without endings, major medical centers are never truly finished. The changing needs of their service populations, evolving health care management and regulatory policies, and advances in medical science and technology keep these large and complex facilities in ongoing planning, design and construction. Updating a great campus is thus a formidable job that Loebl Schlossman & Hackl is honored to fulfill through years of service to Chicago's Resurrection Medical Center. What follows here is a sampling of the projects from Loebl Schlossman & Hackl that expand and modernize the Center, including the Professional Office Building, Main Hospital Entrance, Health & Fitness Center, Second

Floor Nursing Unit, Radiology Department and Dining Facility. As the cornerstone of Resurrection's modernization program, the 160,000-square foot Professional Office Building shifts the Center's primary focus to outpatient services. The new Main Hospital Entrance provides an attractive and functional front door for the Center. A renovation enables the 5,500-square foot Health & Fitness Center to attract and increase employee and community use. The refurbished 27,180-square foot Second Floor Nursing Unit features a new nurses' station, free-standing modular stations, and upgraded patient rooms and corridors. The Radiology Department's 13,950-square foot renovation

Above: Main hospital entrance.
Right: Second floor nurses' station.
Below right: Health & Fitness Center reception.
Opposite: Professional Office Building.
Photography: Scott McDonald/Hedrich Blessing, Bruce Van Inwegen Photography, Doug Snower Photography.

and expansion central-
izes a fragmented
group for greater effi-
ciency and improved
service. Whatever
challenges the future
holds, Resurrection
Medical Center can
now face them with a
21st century facility.

Above left: *Radiology
Department reception.*
Above right: *Dining
facility.*
Right: *Radiology
Department imaging
unit.*

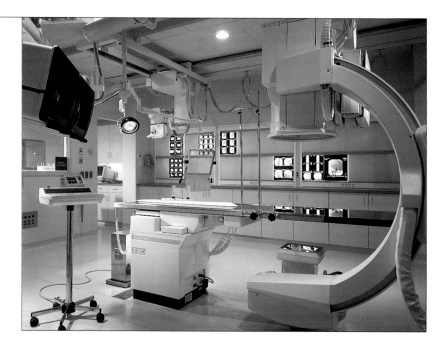

Loebl Schlossman & Hackl

Rehabilitation Institute of Chicago
Chicago, Illinois and Northbrook, Illinois

Ranked by the profession in *U.S. News & World Report* as America's top rehabilitation hospital for eight consecutive years, the Rehabilitation Institute of Chicago retained Loebl Schlossman & Hackl as prime architect with Eva Maddox Associates as consulting architect for design to "rehabilitate" its aging, 360,000-square foot, 19-story facility in Chicago, placing the patient's own motivation at the center of successful rehabilitation. In the 10,000-square foot satellite facility in Northbrook, Illinois, designed by Loebl Schlossman & Hackl, physical, speech and occupational therapy services are provided in teaching patients how to function at home. Clearly RIC intends to retain its ranking.

Above right: *Inpatient rehab gym, Northbrook.*
Right: *Patient floor, Chicago.*
Photography: *Bruce Van Inwegen Photography, Mark Ballogg, Steinkamp/ Ballogg Photography.*

Loebl Schlossman & Hackl

Gottlieb Memorial Hospital
Marjorie G. Weinberg Cancer Care Center
Melrose Park, Illinois

Deliberately contradicting the unsettling public image of cancer, the 14,400-square foot, free-standing Marjorie G. Weinberg Cancer Care Center at Gottlieb Memorial Hospital in Melrose Park, Illinois establishes an airy, peaceful and patient-friendly setting for one of the most technologically advanced facilities of its kind, offering medical and radiation therapy, through an award-winning design by Loebl Schlossman & Hackl. A focal point of the Weinberg Center's planning is the placement of medical oncology adjacent to the exterior glass wall so patients can enjoy outdoor views during their lengthy treatments. Details like this make the facility, which includes a 6 MEV linear accelerator, simulation equipment, eight-room clinic, radiation treatment support areas, consultation space, multiple entrances and waiting room, an encouraging model for cancer care centers to come.

Loebl Schlossman & Hackl

**Weinberg Community
Health Center
Greater Baltimore
Medical Center
Baltimore, Maryland**

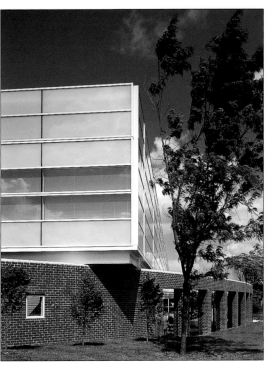

Log onto eBay's online auction site and you will discover how the past lingers in the present. Not everything old can be saved, however. Because renovation of a 30-year-old Community Health Center in a Baltimore inner city neighborhood was impractical, the Greater Baltimore Medical Center has replaced it with the new, 32,000-square foot, two-story Weinberg Community Health Center, designed by Loebl Schlossman & Hackl. The new facility accommodates such activities as pediatrics, radiology/mammography, dental, medical, clinical lab, optical shop, pharmacy, mental health/substance abuse, classrooms, day care and medical records. Its family-friendly design, clad in brick at the lower level and glass above, features a landscaped courtyard entrance that makes the Center resemble a garden where children safely play and adults find valuable resources.

Above left: Masonry wall and glass curtain wall detail.
Above right: Entrance lobby.
Left: Exterior.
Photography: Allan Karchmer.

143

Loebl Schlossman & Hackl

Cook County Hospital Replacement Facility Chicago, Illinois

Generations of Chicagoans have looked to Cook County Hospital for quality care since it opened in 1912. However, extensive studies concluded that the oldest public hospital in the nation could no longer keep pace with changes in health care delivery. So when the CCH Design Group, headed by Loebl Schlossman & Hackl, designed the 1.185 million-square-foot, 464-bed replacement hospital—containing outpatient facilities, obstetrics and pediatric care, emergency/trauma, diagnostic imaging, ancillary services, ambulatory care clinics, surgery department and dietary space—it established optimum patient care and financial performance as its goals. Consequently, the new Cook County Hospital is so efficient it provides better care at less cost, enhancing its relationships with the medical community and patients alike, and assuring this venerable institution a bright future in the Windy City.

Above: Siting of hospital.
Right: Principal elevation.
Photography: James Steinkamp/Steinkamp/ Ballogg Photography.

Matthei & Colin Associates

332 South Michigan Avenue
Suite 614
Chicago
Illinois 60604
312.939.4002
312.939.8164 (Fax)
www.mca-architecture.com
design@mca-architecture.com

Matthei & Colin Associates

Holland Community Hospital
Ambulatory Care Addition
Holland, Michigan

The problem facing Holland, Michigan would sound familiar to countless other communities: Where do you locate a new, much needed ambulatory care facility when the available site is already crowded? For Holland Community Hospital, the prospect was complicated by such needs as lean operations to support the local business community, replacement capacity for existing at-grade parking, and a consolidation of ambulatory services overall. Fortunately, the new, 65,000-square foot, two-level Ambulatory Care Addition, designed by Matthei & Colin Associates, resolves these issues by organizing outpatient services along an outpatient spine with expanded emergency care and diagnostic imaging facilities, relocating the main hospital entrance and erecting a helipad and 102,250-square foot parking deck for 242 cars. Everything is located for maximum efficiency and comfort, including new ORs positioned next to renovated surgical support space, added trauma/treatment bays and urgent care rooms in the newly rearranged emergency department, and better separation and privacy features for staff and public who are happily praising the new facility.

Above: Emergency department.
Right: Entrance at parking deck.
Opposite: Emergency/Radiology entry.
Photography: George Lambros.

Matthei & Colin Associates

Hope Children's Hospital
Advocate Christ Medical Center
Oak Lawn, Illinois

Top left: *Reception.*
Right: *Nurses station.*
Above: *Chapel.*
Opposite: *Entrance and canopy.*
Photography: *George Lambros.*

Children's health care facilities are steadily improving, thanks to new construction across the nation typified by Advocate Christ Medical Center, Oak Lawn, Illinois. The development of the112,000-square foot Hope Children's Hospital, designed by Matthei & Colin Associates, helped the Center resolve two key problems. First, there was insufficient privacy, treatment rooms, support space for family members and equipment

storage. Second, the new institution needed a separate identity while sharing services and power from the main hospital to maintain a tight schedule and modest budget. The patient-focused solution provides 45 private inpatient rooms with their own bathrooms and shower, facilities for family members to stay overnight, separate treatment areas and patient play areas, efficient nurses stations, 15-bed pediatric ICU, outpatient center includ-

ing pediatric rehabilitation, specialty clinics, oncology and cardiology, pediatric radiology, cafeteria, gift shop, chapel and office space, all enveloped by distinctive architecture featuring a curved tensile canopy at the entrance that beckons children and families like a friendly circus tent.

Edward Hospital
Expansion for Women's & Children's Center
Naperville, Illinois

How do health care administrators respond to an influx of young families in their community? Facing a rapidly growing population whose demand for women's and children's health care services is rising accordingly, Edward Hospital, in Naperville, Illinois, recently expanded its Women's & Children's Center with a design by Matthei & Colin Associates. The new, 94,000-square foot, three-story addition, encompassing an 18-LDR and 36-bed post-partum unit, a women's diagnostic care center with facilities for the treatment of battered women and children, and an expanded radiology department with a mammography and ultrasound suite, establishes an identifiable access point for its services. In addition, it joins the surrounding complex of medical office buildings and parking structures to the main hospital with a new enclosed pedestrian link and a new outpatient entrance and lobby that greet patients with such amenities as a fireplace, aquarium, player piano, coffee shop and—for those who aren't too preoccupied to look—sweeping views of the outdoor fountain and landscaping.

Above: *Outpatient Garden.*
Below: *South lobby.*
Opposite: *Thee story atrium.*
Photography: *Wayne Cable.*

Matthei & Colin Associates

Ravenswood Hospital Medical Center
Advocate Health Care
Community Health Resource Center
Chicago, Illinois

Above left: *Exterior.*
Above right: *Lobby clerestory and ceiling.*
Left: *Lobby*
Photography: *George Lambros.*

Thinking of outpatients as customers, Chicago's Ravenswood Hospital has reached to capture new markets and retain existing ones using modular Community Health Resource Centers designed by Matthei & Colin Associates. Each of two completed Centers, at 25,300 square feet and 36,000 square feet, includes such diagnostic services as ultrasound, mammography and laboratory, patient education, administration and community support space. The convenient, cost-effective and attractive facilities provide exam/treatment "pod" configurations with swing space to manage patient volume fluctuations, centralized payment and scheduling that reduce staffing requirements, and abundant daylight and neighborhood views, features that should appeal to the customer in each of us.

MGE Architects

150 Alhambra Circle
Suite 700
Coral Gables
Florida 33134

7251 West Palmetto Road
Suite 102
Boca Raton
Florida 33433

305.444.0413
www.mgearchitects.com

MGE Architects
Lois Pope LIFE Center
University of Miami School of Medicine
Miami, Florida

The Miami Project to Cure Paralysis at the University of Miami School of Medicine, Miami, Florida, is the world's largest, most comprehensive research center dedicated to finding more effective treatments and ultimately a cure for paralysis resulting from spinal cord injury. Founded in 1985 by Dr. Barth Green, an expert in the field, the Miami Project recently assembled its researchers, clinicians and therapists under one roof, following the completion of the 115,000-square foot, seven-story Lois Pope LIFE Center, designed by MGE Architects. The facility employs the research laboratory floor as its primary building block, using an open, modular laboratory concept from Garikes, Wilson, Karlsberger to encourage collaboration and interaction among the staff. In the overall scheme, meeting rooms are centrally located, break out areas are vertically integrated, and circulation is directed between wet lab benches and dry work stations organized in laboratory pods flooded with daylight and views. The seventh-floor Apex Conference Center, a fixed seating media center, is designed to make major research conferences thrive here as much as the research that supports them.

Above: Exterior.
Right: Apex Conference Center auditorium.
Photography: Steven Brooke Studios.

154

Top: Laboratory.
Above: Main lobby.
Right: Office/breakout area.

Boca Raton Community Hospital
Boca Raton, Florida

Left: *Outpatient Diagnostic Center lobby.*
Above: *Toppel Center.*
Photography: *Patricia Fisher.*

Below: Reception area, John Henry Mind/Body Center.
Bottom left: LDRP room.
Bottom right: Emergency department.

It's interesting to see how young and old residents of Boca Raton, Florida are driving the ongoing program of renovations, additions and new freestanding construction at Boca Raton Community Hospital, designed by MGE Architects. The work implements a master plan that the architects completed for the hospital in 1993 to provide needed updating and new services while maintaining its high image. Included thus far have been such facilities as a 10-bed CCU, new main entrance with lobby and admissions, 12-bed LDRP with C-section rooms and nursery, radiotherapy department with two linear accelerators, cath lab, ultrasound and nuclear medicine diag-

nostic expansion, 14-station hemodialysis unit and freestanding central stores and plan operations building, campus outpatient center, MRI, and sports medicine and cardiac rehabilitation facilities. While Boca Raton Community Hospital may never stop revising and expanding itself, the people of Boca Raton will never doubt that it is prepared for whatever their needs may be.

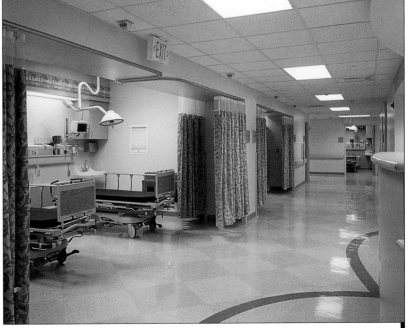

**Joe DiMaggio Children's Hospital
Pediatric ICU/Medical Surgical Suites
Hollywood, Florida**

Converting a fourth floor wing of Joe DiMaggio Children's Hospital, Hollywood, Florida, into a 15,000-square foot, 22-bed pediatric ICU and medical surgery unit, designed by MGE Architects, set the stage for comprehensive care that benefits patients, siblings, parents and staff alike. For example, the facility's central core of nursing support is efficient for staff because it can be shared by up to four nursing work area pods, depending on patient census. Each pod in turn has visual and computerized patient monitoring capability with clear sight lines to all patient rooms, which allow doctors and nurses to perform all procedures at patients' bedsides, and incorporate family pantries and overnight sleepers to encourage family participation. As a finishing touch, the visual themes of baseball and home life in the tropics coax smiles from the boys and girls loved by the former Yankee baseball star.

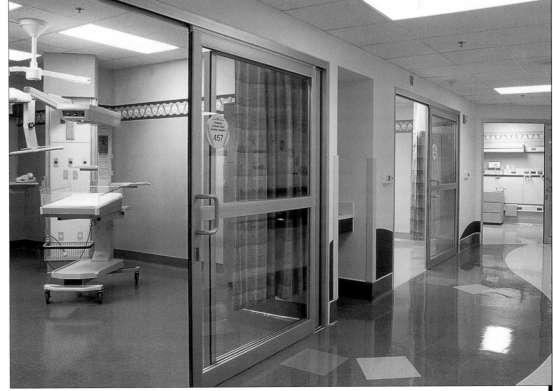

Above: *Exterior.*
Right: *Pediatric ICU.*
Opposite above:
Nurses station hallway.
Opposite below:
Children's play room.
Photography: *Patricia Fisher.*

MGE Architects **Holy Cross Hospital**
Michael and Diane Bienes Comprehensive Cancer Center
The Jim Moran Cardiovascular Center
Ft. Lauderdale, Florida

You sense a difference in the 23,000-square foot addition to the Michael and Diane Bienes Comprehensive Cancer Center at Holy Cross Hospital, Ft. Lauderdale, Florida, designed by MGE Architects, when you leave the elevator to enter a library doubling as reception and waiting room. Built above the existing Center, the expansion offers contemporary furnishings and daylight to put patients at ease. Its diagnostic and treatment space is segmented into a physicians' area, zoned for patient convenience and staff privacy, and an infusion therapy area, a landscaped room that alleviates patients' stress. The Hospital's new, 90,000-square foot Heart Center medical office building, also designed by MGE Architects, celebrates its own individuality with a wellness center and heart health cafe.

Above: Reception and waiting room in Cardiovascular Center.
Photography: Patricia Fisher.

Upper right: Exterior of Cardiovascular Center.
Center: Infusion therapy area in Cancer Center.
Lower right: Waiting room in Cancer Center.

NBBJ

1555 Lake Shore Drive
Columbus
Ohio 43204
614.224.7145
614.224.0268 (Fax)

111 S. Jackson Street
Seattle
Washington 98104
206.223.5555
206.621.2314 (Fax)

www.nbbj.com
health@nbbj.com

London
Los Angeles
New York
Oslo
Raleigh
San Francisco
Taipei
Tokyo

Swedish Medical Center
Southeast Tower Addition
Seattle, Washington

Above left: *Lobby Cafe detail.*
Above center: *Chapel.*
Above right: *Nurses station.*
Below: *OR recovery beds.*
Opposite: *Corridor.*
Photography: *Farshid Assassi, Steve Keating, Russell Johnson.*

Satisfying patients has been raised to an art at the award-winning, 671,000-square foot, nine-story East Tower Addition at Swedish Medical Center in Seattle, Washington. Designed by NBBJ, the tower establishes a landmark identity, signifying the Center's forward-looking character and regional prominence. Uniting the existing buildings creates a functional entrance and transforms the acute care hospital into an ambulatory care center. Inside, interiors feel warm and friendly to patients, families and visitors without diminishing the importance of advanced technology to the medical profession. The varied facilities reflect a timeless quality of lightness, freshness and optimism. Breaking from convention, their spaces honor the human spirit using such elements as curvilinear spaces, naturally finished wood trim, cabinetry and surfaces, soothing colors, subtle lighting, abundant views and art from regional artists—a patient-friendly vision of the Pacific Northwest. The Center's commitment to art as a way to expand patients' horizons, bolster their confidence and help them find the strength to survive, both physically and spiritually, dates back to its pursuit of healing design in the 1970s. Dr. Alan Lobb, a prominent surgeon, noted local sculptor and CEO of the Center, made art an integral component of the Center's healing environment by welcoming the work of such distinguished Northwest artists as Horiuchi, Tobey, Anderson and Tsutikawa inside its walls. Today, the Tower's original and commissioned art proudly reaffirms this enlightened commitment.

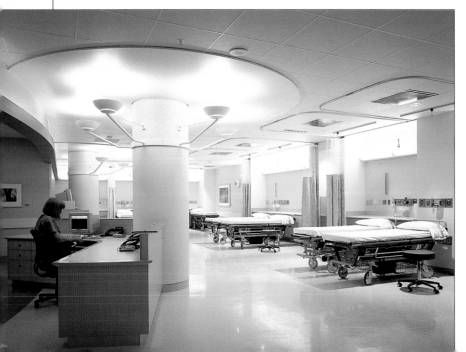

Woodwinds Health Campus
Woodbury, Minnesota

Below: *Towne Center.*
Photography: *Paul Warchol.*

While a hospital can never be a home or hotel, creative opportunities exist within every facility to capture the feelings or the essence of a hospitality environment. A splendid example is Woodwinds Health Campus located in Woodbury, Minnesota, designed by NBBJ. Woodwinds encompasses a 70-bed, 148,000-square foot hospital and 90,000-square foot medical office building. As the first major hospital built beyond city limits for one of the Twin Cities' fastest-growing communities, Woodwinds enhances healing through a design that consciously harmonizes with nature, beginning with its site of pristine woodlands and wetlands. Other aspects of this unique approach are a building form that maximizes daylight and views for all family spaces, inpatient rooms and holding areas. The interior environment features indigenous natural building materials and museum quality local craftsmanship. Fireplaces, coffee shops, nature trails and a chapel offer choices for patients, families and staff that reinforce the concept of a unique and memorable health care experience.

Above: *Family day room intensive care unit (ICU).*
Below left: *Patient room.*
Below right: *Inpatient corridor and nurses station.*

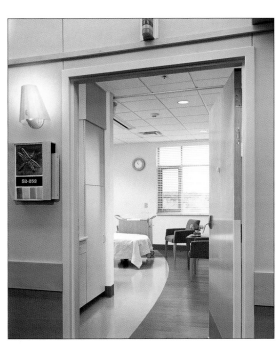

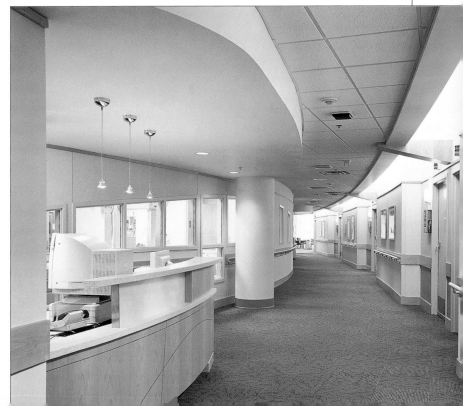

NBBJ

Rainbow Babies and Childrens Hospital
Horvitz Tower
University Hospitals of Cleveland
Cleveland, Ohio

How would a hospital look if a child designed it? The primary goal of Cleveland's Rainbow Babies and Childrens Hospital has been to provide a positive, enabling environment that supports the physical, social and developmental needs of the child and family. In fact, capturing the child's imagination and encouraging feelings of comfort, control and discovery produce an exceptional environment. Consequently, NBBJ designed this nationally respected pediatric medical center's new 280,000-square foot, eight-story bedtower addition. At its heart is a wayfinding concept employing the colors of the rainbow and such themes as games, arts, transportation, science and industry, which are depicted as abstract, cartoon-like icons throughout the facility. This concept is reinforced by an efficient floor plan featuring three nursing clusters. Each pod supports ten patient rooms and includes a core of share services. The private patient rooms include fold-out couches for parents, art walls for children and spacious staff work areas. This design reinforces the client's commitment to family centered care. Undoubtedly, the children will probably focus on the smiling whales, sleek oceanliners and other reminders that Rainbow Babies sees the world as they do.

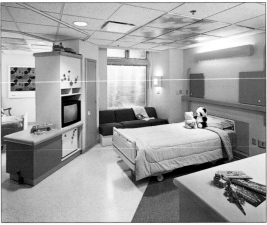

Alaska Native Medical Center
Anchorage, Alaska

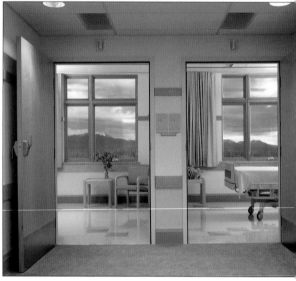

Left: Lobby.
Above: Clinical spaces.
Top: Meditation room.
Photography: Farshid Assassi.

Providing advanced medical care for Alaska's small villages includes more than 150 acute care beds, a 59-bed hostel and the Centers for Disease Control Arctic Investigations Laboratory. Designed by NBBJ, the 380,635-square foot Alaska Native Medical Center in Anchorage is the largest project ever undertaken by the U.S. Public Health Service, and accommodates Aleuts, Eskimos, and Indians of seven distinct native cultures. Emphasizing the shared values that bind these people, the facility creates a hierarchy of gathering spaces based on traditional geometries that reinforce family and community, promoting the physical and spiritual healing of all native Alaskans.

OWP/P

111 West Washington Street
Suite 2100
Chicago
Illinois 60602.2714
312.332.9600
312.332.9601 (Fax)
www.owpp.com

OWP/P

Northwest Community Healthcare
North Pavilion
Arlington Heights, Illinois

Left: *Entrance exterior.*
Lower left: *Family waiting area in CCU.*
Bottom left: *Lobby with piano.*
Bottom right: *Surgical preparation area.*
Opposite: *Meditation room.*
Photography: *Doug Snower (exterior), Hedrich Blessing (interior).*

An exceptional health care environment that actively supports the triad of care—patient, family and caregiver—draws everyone's attention at the new, 133,000-square foot, three-floor North Pavilion of Northwest Community Healthcare, Arlington Heights, Illinois, designed by OWP/P. The award-winning facility welcomes family involvement at many points during a patient's stay. It's a complex space, housing such accommodations as a patient entrance and centralized registration, surgical family waiting area, 11-OR surgical suite, four-room endoscopy suite, 17-bed post-anesthesia unit, 36-bed critical care unit, central sterile supply and such amenities as a cafe and meditation room. To aid healing, the design connects to nature through the cafe flower garden, organic forms, natural light and a variety of textures, and is further supported by a piano in the lobby, a lounge in the pre-op/endoscopy unit with children's play areas, residential-style furnishings and indirect lighting. Mark Lusson, NWCH vice president recently commented, "It is what we hoped could be developed when we set out on this project."

University of Chicago Hospitals
Duchossois Center for Advanced Medicine
Chicago, Illinois

Chicagoans respect the University of Chicago Hospitals for its tradition, quality and commitment to exceptional service, and the new, 525,000-square foot, seven-story Duchossois Center for Advanced Medicine, with interior design by OWP/P, reaffirms their trust. The interior spaces, encompassing diagnostic and treatment services on the lower three floors and clinical services on floors 4-6, are designed to accommodate the needs of outpatients and withstand heavy wear. Yet they also take care to establish a human scale in clinical areas, which are designed as modules with physicians' work areas for conferences between attending physicians and house staff as well as standard design features for relatively straightforward reassignment. These and other provisions, such as space plans that limit patient travel to 300 feet or less, a corridor system separating staff and materials from patients, waiting areas with windows or atrium exposure, and such amenities as a lounge, dining room, gift shop and pharmacy, help ensure a visit to the Center is a dignified and meaningful experience.

Above: Reception desk and waiting area.
Right: Main lobby.
Opposite: Elevator lobby.
Photography: Steve Hall/Hedrich Blessing.

Silver Cross Hospital
Arthur and Vera Smith Pavilion
Joliet, Illinois

Upper left: *Healing garden.*
Left: *Cafeteria.*
Lower left: *Intensive care unit.*
Photography: *Doug Snower, Paul Schlismann (ICU).*

Above: *Exterior at new main entrance.*

Nobody doubted Silver Cross Hospital, Joliet, Illinois, would benefit from a central location for surgery. But as OWP/P knew, turning an inspiration into a 101,553-square foot, three-story addition, the Arthur and Vera Smith Pavilion, resembled surgery itself. First, there were functions to incorporate, including outpatient neurosurgery, orthopedic and minimally-invasive surgery, outpatient diagnostics, dialysis unit, nuclear medicine, ICU, sterile processing, healing garden, new main entrance, registration/ office, gift shop, cafeteria, pre-op holding/post-op recovery, prep/recovery area and pre-op stage 2 recovery. Then, existing buildings needed connections on 13 different elevations using level interfaces and ramps. Last but not least, patients received a healing environment with generous spaces, good wayfinding, natural light, attractive, contemporary furnishings and a healing garden—letting a complex building simplify surgery for patients, families and staff.

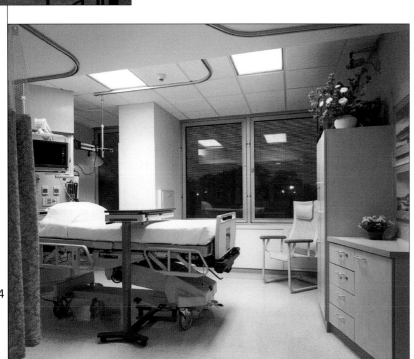

OWP/P

University of Illinois at Chicago Hospital Craniofacial Center
Chicago, Illinois

Above: Soffit detail in corridor.
Right: Pediatric waiting area.
Below: Treatment room and office.
Photography: Chris Barrett/Hedrich Blessing.

Many patients with craniofacial anomalies arrive for treatment at the University of Illinois at Chicago Hospital, in Chicago, Illinois, with visual and perceptual difficulties. So when OWP/P began the recent renovation of the 15,400-square foot Craniofacial Center, it focused on maximizing efficiency and wayfinding to help pediatric and adult patients alike. To begin, spaces were planned to reflect a patient visiting sequence driven by specialties. This created adjacencies based on convenience and a high level of integration for such multidisciplinary diagnostic and therapeutic spaces as maxiofacial surgery, dentistry, psychology, speech therapy and genetics. Playful shapes and forms were dressed in bright colors and exposed to natural light wherever possible to provide orientational cues that patients could comprehend during stays that would often run for many hours. The result is an environment that is truly easy on the eyes.

Right: Northwestern
Memorial Hospital
Olson Pavilion.
Below: LithoLink.
Photography:
Paul Schlismann
Photography.

As the sciences prolifer-
ate in a multitude of
new directions and at
unprecedented velocities
of change, architects of
laboratories keep pace
by collecting as much
empirical data as possi-
ble, drawing intuition
from experience, and
applying information as
widely as they can. Thus,
OWP/P, which has pro-
vided architectural and
engineering services on
hundreds of thousands
of square feet of lab
space for health care,
higher education and
the corporate world,
regards lab design as a
work in perpetual
progress. Whatever
drives today's lab
design—such as comput-
ers, cleanliness, flexibility
for technology and peo-
ple and above all, the
evolving scientific
process—OWP/P provides
innovative solutions at
every opportunity.

Paul Finch & Associates, P.C.

3550 Buckner Boulevard
Virginia Beach
Virginia 23456
754.471.0537
754.471.4205 (Fax)
www.pfa-architect.com

Paul Finch & Associates. P.C.

W. Stanley Jennings
Outpatient Center
Chesapeake General Hospital
Chesapeake, Virginia

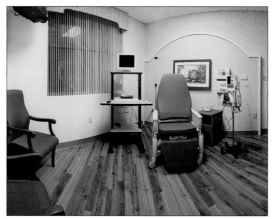

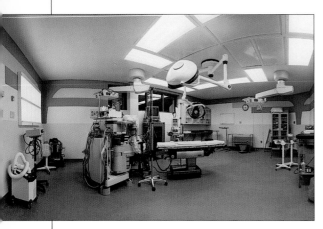

Above left: *Operating room.*
Above right: *Healing garden.*
Upper left: *Reception desk.*
Upper right:
Pre-op/post-op room.

Above: *Exterior at entrance.*
Photography: *Gene Woolridge, Advertising Visuals.*

Outpatient surgery includes surgical procedures which do not require overnight hospitalization. This type of surgery is so popular at Chesapeake General Hospital, Chesapeake, Virginia, that it spurred the development of the new 38,000-square foot, two-story W. Stanley Jennings Outpatient Center, designed by Paul Finch & Associates. The Center's highlights include an Urgent Care Center with 10 exam rooms, procedure room and x-ray facilities; Diagnostic Area with 3 EKGs and laboratory; and Outpatient Surgery with 14 private pre-op/post-op rooms and 4 ORs. Besides creating a sophisticated facility dramatized by a 38-foot-high glass spline separating Recovery/Urgent Care from Surgery/Diagnostic, the designers envelope patients in a graceful, stress-reducing environment of abundant natural light, wood accents and a healing garden with fish pond and waterfall. Not surprisingly, this project recently received a national award from the Center for Innovation in Health Facilities, designating this building as one of America's top 10 health care facilities.

Paul Finch & Associates. P.C.

Cancer Treatment Center
Chesapeake General Hospital
Chesapeake, Virginia

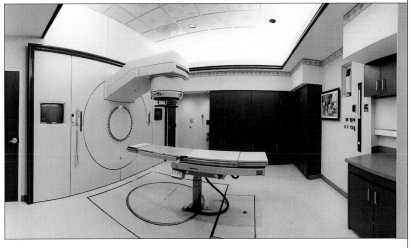

Above: Linear accelerator room.

Because of the unique demands that cancer surgery, chemotherapy and radiation therapy impose on medical staff and patients, cancer centers tend to be unique among health care facilities. Not only is treatment stressful to patients, working with cancer patients is debilitating to staff. Taking these concerns to heart, Chesapeake General Hospital, Chesapeake, Virginia, retained Paul Finch & Associates to design its 6,245-square foot, state-of-the-art Cancer Treatment Center as a warm, residential-style environment. Consequently, the floor plan separates patient and staff flows to appear less clinical to patients, while natural light streams in from skylights and clerestory windows to introduce an airy atmosphere. A complementary image is sustained in the lobby/waiting, reception, offices, linear accelerator, exam rooms, dressing rooms and other accommodations through comfortable, contemporary furniture, carpet and wallcoverings in soothing colors, dark wood trim, an aquarium and other residential-style furnishings. As a result, Rebecca W. Maples, Chesapeake General's vice president, planning and marketing recently noted, "The medical director is delighted with the facility and its user-friendly qualities."

Paul Finch & Associates. P.C.   Wayfinding
Sentara Virginia Beach General Hospital
Virginia Beach, Virginia

Above: *Information desk.*
Photography: *Gene Woolridge, Advertising Visuals.*

Hospitals are like growing families who find organization gets harder as their numbers increase. The arrival of one addition after another can so complicate hospital operations, wayfinding and identity that renovations become unavoidable. For Sentara Virginia Beach General Hospital, Virginia Beach, Virginia, a recent, 8,435-square foot, award-winning renovation, designed by Paul Finch & Associates, has proven to be the right prescription. The hospital needed a hierarchy of spaces that staff and the public could immediately comprehend, so that the main entry and principal destinations would be readily identifiable, interior pedestrian routes would be efficient and navigable, public/patient, semi-public and staff/private areas would be clearly separated, and arrival queues would be easily established. In response, the designers remodeled the reception area and information desk, and introduced information kiosks, maps, signage, planters and palettes of finishes featuring marble, vinyl, carpet, wood and laminate in warm and inviting tones as part of a far-reaching and accessible visual language that anyone in the hospital—regardless of family size—can understand.

Left: *Entrance to cardiology and peripheral vascular lab.*
Below left: *Windows along corridor.*
Bottom: *Outpatient pharmacy.*

Paul Finch & Associates. P.C.   St. Mary's Home for Disabled Children
Norfolk, Virginia

Making children feel at home in an institution is never easy, and the task is complicated by the special needs of the children destined for the new, 83,251-square foot St. Mary's Home for Disabled Children, Norfolk, Virginia, designed by Paul Finch & Associates. St. Mary's is an intermediate care facility for mentally retarded children (ICF/MR) ranging in age from birth to 18 years that is dedicated to enhancing the children's lives and reassuring their parents. When it is completed, the brick and glass structure under an aluminum standing seam roof will deliberately evoke the form of a small town. Through a central spine ("sidewalk") of courtyards surrounded by active treatment rooms ("school") and patient pods ("home") anchored by a circular activity room ("town center"), St. Mary's will nurture a community as special as its residents.

Above: A wing extending from the central spine.
Right: Courtyard adjacent to the circular activity room.
Below: Elevation along main axis.

Perkins Eastman Architects PC

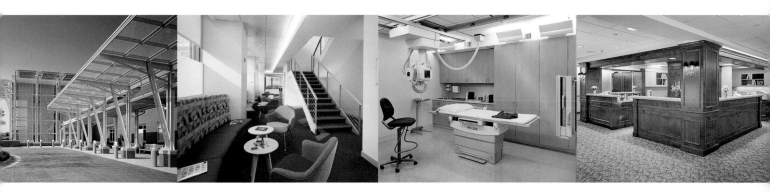

115 Fifth Avenue
New York
New York 10003
212.353.7200
212.353.7676 (Fax)
www.peapc.com
info@peapc.com

Charlotte
Pittsburgh
Stamford
Toronto

Perkins Eastman Architects PC   University of Arkansas Medical Sciences Donald W. Reynolds Center on Aging Little Rock, Arkansas

The Donald W. Reynolds Center on Aging represents one of the first facilities in the country to create an interdisciplinary home for gerontology programs in patient services, clinical research, basic science research, public policy and education. Reliance on state-of-the-art technology to connect the University of Arkansas' new center with other educational sites around the world, and a clear mission to bring researchers, educators, students, and patients together, guided the design of this award-winning facility. Two complementary components, a north volume serving research and education and a south volume serving patients and visitors, are bisected by a linear spine or atrium. These spaces offer the community of users a richly varied environment with contemporary, durable furnishings in attractive, airy and well-lit spaces. This combination of

physical and technological features has positioned the Center on Aging to play a major role in shaping the next generation of treatments and caregivers for older adults. Commented Dr. David A. Lipschitz, director of the Center on Aging and chairman of the Geriatrics Department, "It's a truly remarkable facility."

Upper right: *Reception and waiting area.*
Right: *Auditorium.*
Below: *Exterior.*
Opposite: *Linear spine or atrium.*
Photography: *Tim Hursley/The Arkansas Office.*

Perkins Eastman Architects PC

New York University
Child Care Study Center
New York, New York

"Children and fools cannot lie," noted John Heywood, 16th-century English anthologist of colloquial sayings. Keeping faith with children is serious business for the 17,000-square foot, two-level Child Care Study Center at New York University. Serving children with potential psychiatric problems, the Center cultivates a welcoming, non-institutional character to appeal to them without condescension. Though originally constructed to residential specifications (low ceilings), the Center overcame its spatial restrictions, integrating contemporary furnishings, indirect lighting and carefully routed ductwork throughout into a design which reflects the allure of casual clothing retailers. Children might say the Center is bright, playful and engaging—but not childish.

Above: Conference area lounge.
Left: Reception desk.
Right: Medical offices.
Opposite: Waiting room.
Photography: Chuck Choi.

Perkins Eastman Architects PC

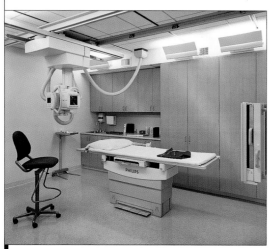

In a classic, New York City transformation from ugly duckling to swan, a mundane 1970s office building recently re-emerged as the 200,000-square foot, 11-story Laurance S. Rockefeller Outpatient Pavilion, designed by Perkins Eastman Architects. This facility is the flagship of Memorial Sloan-Kettering's off-campus ambulatory care network. Its design incorporates a patient friendly floorplate with a central reception and registration area, serving a diagnostic suite to one side and a chemotherapy suite to the other. It is enriched with fountains, information carrels, and self-service refreshment areas, and is differentiated floor by floor with various architectural elements and interior finishes. It successfully balances both uniformity and diversity into a warm and friendly healthcare facility—so much so that patients balk at visiting more institutional settings for treatment.

Top left: Reception area.
Upper left: Chemotherapy suite.
Left: Diagnostic room.
Right: Registration area.
Photography: Chuck Choi.

Laurance S. Rockefeller Outpatient Pavilion
Memorial Sloan-Kettering Cancer Center
New York, New York

Perkins Eastman Architects PC

Special Patients Unit
Memorial Sloan-Kettering Cancer Center
New York, New York

More than a few inpatients may dream that their hospital rooms were hotel rooms. However, patients with special needs for supplemental accommodations, security and privacy can regard the new, 18,000-square foot Special Patients Unit, as a dream come true. Although its 14 patient care units, supported by common, medical and staff areas, meet the code and maintenance requirements of a hospital, they resemble four-star hotels. The units include deluxe rooms and two room suites equipped with sleeping sofas, refrigerators, facsimile/copiers and entertainment systems. Common areas include a lounge and library; the front desk provides security and concierge services. Although gracious. their appearance masks an inner strength. Carpeting uses solution-dyed nylon with a solid vinyl backing for moisture tightness; type II vinyl wallcovering combines toughness with cleanability; custom millwork and furniture are treated with finishes resistant to harsh disinfectants and cleaners; and luxurious upholstery is easily cleaned synthetic leather or removable slipcovers. Naturally, the robes, linens and tableware are custom-designed as well.

Upper left: *Patient lounge and library.*
Upper right: *Private bathroom.*
Lower left: *Patient room.*
Lower right: *Nurses station.*
Photography: *Chuck Choi.*

Perkins & Will

800.837.9455
healthcare@perkinswill.com
www.perkinswill.com

Atlanta
Boston
Charlotte
Chicago
Dallas
Los Angeles
Miami
Minneapolis
Research Triangle Park

Perkins & Will

Cedars-Sinai
Ambulatory Care Center Relocation
Los Angeles, California

There was considerable user resistance to moving Cedars-Sinai Ambulatory Care Center in Los Angeles. It's easy to see why, given Perkins & Will's assignment to transform a 40,000-square foot former warehouse with virtually no windows, little street presence and not even a "front door" into a user-friendly health care facility. However, maximizing the natural light from the small amount of window area, keeping the functional layout of the clinics modular for future flexibility, and orienting everything with a central lobby and "gate house" that bring pedestrians from the ground level to the principal space on the upper level has changed everything. The new clinics for pediatrics, adult/OB, dental, wound and employee health, as well as the diabetes education center, procedure center and satellite pharmacy, proved so appealing that the users couldn't wait to move in—and often say they can't believe the transformation.

Perkins & Will

Midstate Medical Center
Meriden, Connecticut

Left: *Exterior.*
Opposite: *Galleria.*
Below left: *Patient corridor with decentralized nursing.*
Below right: *Cafeteria.*
Photography: *Peter Mauss/Esto Photographics (exterior), Scott McDonald @ Hedrich Blessing (interior).*

Health care planners are learning that in unity there can be financial strength. In 1995, the State of Connecticut permitted Veterans Memorial Medical Center, Meriden-Wallingford Community Corporation, Hartford Hospital and Connecticut Health System, Inc. to streamline the operations of two aging facilities with 354 beds by constructing New England's first new standalone hospital in two decades. MidState Medical Center is a 237,000-square foot, 92-bed replacement hospital designed by Perkins & Will on a 50-acre site in Meriden. Developed simultaneously with an operational re-engineering program, MidState establishes an outpatient-focused facility with advanced technology and a prominent public image. It groups program elements into three distinct components: the diagnostic and treatment block, the medical office building and the patient care pavilions. A "main street" or galleria acts as MidState's main public circulation spine, while a "town green" creates a ceremonial and functional entry forecourt. The subtle balance it maintains between civic importance and patient-friendly intimacy befits its New England community.

Perkins & Will

Heartland Medical Center
Sebring, Florida

Left: *Exterior.*
Below left: *Entrance.*
Opposite: *Public hall.*
Photography: *Jonathan Hillyer, (left and below left); Gabriel Benzur (opposite).*

One of the most successful health care facilities in the Adventist Healthcare System is Heartland Medical Center, Sebring, Florida, designed by Perkins & Will. The 235,000-square foot, three-story facility is anchored by a 400-foot long, two-story high public hall connecting such major components as administration, surgery, inpatient and outpatient areas, doctors' offices, laboratories, library, conference center, meeting rooms, wellness center, women's services, food servery/dining, retail space, exhibit/gallery space and parking. Inspired by a vision that Heartland would be open to the community as a community based wellness center, its planners specifically asked for a hospital that would incorporate staffing efficiency, flexibility for future growth, integration of new technology and a design that was open, light, and non-institutional in character. How the community feels about the hospital was warmly demonstrated at the festive grand opening—attended by over 25,000 residents.

Perkins & Will

Anschutz Cancer Pavilion
University of Colorado
Health Sciences University Hospital, Aurora, CO

Left: *Reception and waiting area.*
Lower left: *Exterior.*
Lower center: *Infusion area.*
Lower right: *Terrace outside infusion area.*
Photography: *Ron Johnson.*

A preview of the academic medical center of the future has opened on a 200-plus-acre campus that was formerly the Fitzsimons Army Garrison, where the Health Sciences Center and University Hospital of the University of Colorado recently completed the 109,000-square foot, three-story Anschutz Cancer Pavilion, designed by Perkins & Will and Davis Partnership. The Cancer Pavilion represents the first of a series of facilities in a master plan developed by Perkins & Will and Davis Partnership that will ultimately include an Eye Institute, Centers for Advanced Medicine and a Research Facility. A warm and comfortable environment designed for easy wayfinding greets patients of the Cancer Pavilion to perimeter public corridors that bring daylight indoors, an infusion area adjacent to an exterior terrace landscaped as a healing garden, and such key facilities as a patient resource center, exam rooms, imaging facilities, lab and radiation oncology. The academic medicine of tomorrow looks decidedly upbeat today in the Rocky Mountain State.

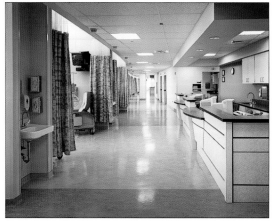

RMW architecture & interiors

160 Pine Street
San Francisco
California 94111
415.781.9800
415.788.5216 (Fax)
info@rmw.com

555 Fifth Street
Suite 200
Santa Rosa
California 95401
707.573.0715
707.573.3056 (Fax)

2601 Blake Street
Suite 400
Denver
Colorado 80205
303.297.9500
303.296.0122 (Fax)

40 South Market Street
4th Floor
San Jose
California 95113
408.294.8000
408.294.1747 (Fax)

1718 Third Street
Suite 101
Sacramento
California 95814
916.449.1400
916.449.1414 (Fax)

www.rmw.com

Palo Alto Medical Foundation
New Campus
Palo Alto, California

Above: *Atrium.*
Left: *Staff entry court.*
Opposite: *Clock tower.*
Photography: *David Wakely.*

The new 7.6 acre integrated medical campus has been designed by RMW to give the Palo Alto Medical Foundation in Palo Alto, California a 258,000 square foot, four-level medical office building, a 37,000 square foot medical research center and a 370,000 square foot, two-level 1,000 car underground parking garage. Established in the 1930s as a multi-specialty medical group, the Foundation is now an affiliate of the Sutter Health System and encompasses a health-care campus serving a regional population through a professional partnership of 200 physicians and 700-plus support staff treating over 120,000 patients annually in Palo Alto, plus others at satellite clinics in Fremont and Los Altos, California. RMW was commissioned to complete the design and planning of the project based upon a concept design by Ellerbe-Becket. The new campus was developed in response to shifting patient demographics, an aggressive medical research program and advancements in diagnostic and treatment equipment technology, which collectively rendered the Foundation's aging clinic

Right: Surgecenter waiting area.
Below left: Plastic and reconstructive surgery procedure room.
Bottom left: Pediatrics reception area.

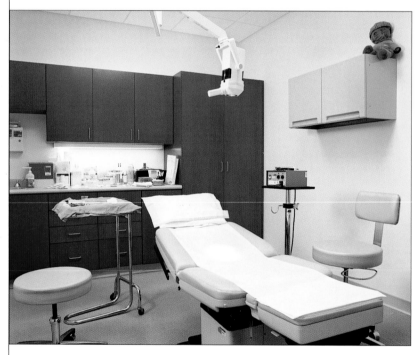

204

facilities obsolete. The broad mission of the facility is evident in the program for the medical office building, which provides primary care, urgent care, outpatient surgery and other specialty clinics, each with its own separate reception and waiting areas. Diagnostic and treatment spaces support the clinic functions and include an imaging department with facilities for CT scan, radiography and MRI; a radiation oncology department with 2 linear accelerators and a simulator; a clinical lab for specimen accessioning and analysis; and an outpatient pharmacy. The remainder of the facility is comprised of administrative support space, a servery and cafeteria adjacent to a sub-dividable conference center providing an auditorium setting for community education and outreach programs. The complex organization of a wide variety of clinical, public and administrative spaces is successfully accomplished in an economical, functional and patient-friendly environment, supported by a simplified way-finding system of graphics, colors and finish materials. In context with its location adjacent to the campus of Stanford University, the Foundation is framed in the region's prevailing Mediterranean style.

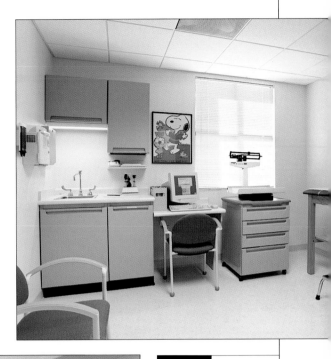

Above: *Pediatrics exam room.*
Left: *Plastic and reconstructive surgery waiting area.*

Palo Alto Medical Foundation
Fremont Medical Office Building
Fremont, California

At ground breaking, the new Fremont Medical Office Building in Fremont, California, an extension of the Palo Alto Medical Foundation, was boldly described as "a center for health and healing." Today, the Foundation's sleek, state-of-the-art, 58,500-square foot, two-story building, designed by RMW, has convincingly fulfilled that pledge. Believing that healthcare providers will increasingly treat patients holistically—maintaining their ongoing wellness rather than merely intervening in episodes of acute illness—the Foundation capitalized on the reputation it enjoys among Fremont's rapidly growing population by creating its own local identity. The new facility offers the services of 230 employees, including 55 physicians in family medicine, internal medicine, pediatrics, OB-GYN, ophthalmology, dermatology, podiatry, psychiatry and other specialties. Its range of spaces, including reception, waiting, doctors' offices, examination and procedure rooms, radiology department, laboratory, medical records area and staff lounge, reflects the Foundation's desire to join streamlined patient management to a humane and comforting environment. Patients quickly feel at ease when they arrive. Each floor has a centrally located reception desk flanked by four waiting areas shared by all departments except for psychiatry, which has one of its own. While doctors' offices line the perime-

Above: Stairwell.
Right: Entrance.
Opposite: Reception desk.
Photography: David Wakely.

ter, examination and procedure rooms stand adjacent to the public areas. The service core is located at the rear of reception and waiting. Sensitive use of a sky-lighted staircase, vaulted ceiling with exposed trusses, contemporary finishes with a residential feel, indirect lighting and attractive, comfortable furniture ensure that patients have a positive experience whenever they visit.

Above: *Waiting area.*
Left: *Entrance at dusk.*

RDLA • Robert D. Lynn Associates

1500 Walnut Street   Bellingham
Suite 1800   Washington
Philadelphia   360.756.1200
Pennsylvania 19102
215.545.8500   Portland
215.545.3012 (Fax)   Oregon
rdl@rdla.com   503.232.8640

Abington Memorial Hospital
Abington, Pennsylvania

Changes in resident populations, medical science and health care administration oblige institutions such as Abington Memorial Hospital, Abington, Pennsylvania, to play endless rounds of catch-up. Such was the case when Abington Memorial recently undertook 385,000 square feet of new construction, 400,000 square feet of structural parking and 55,000 square feet of renovations, designed by Robert D. Lynn Associates. However, the project—including a 26,5000-square foot emergency/ trauma department, 15-OR surgical suite, 42-bed outpatient short procedure unit, 65,000-square foot medical office building and parking for 960 cars—is so skillfully interwoven in new and renovated space that visitors describe the results as "breathtaking."

Left: Toll Pavilion.
Below: Levy Medical Office Building.
Photography: Matt Wargo.

RDLA • Robert D. Lynn Associates

Jonathan Evans Rhoads Pavilion
Hospital of the University of Pennsylvania
Philadelphia, Pennsylvania

Left: *Main lobby.*
Above: *Exterior.*

A recent addition to the University of Pennsylvania Medical Center in Philadelphia, Pennsylvania, the new, 218,000-square foot Jonathan Evans Rhoads Pavilion, designed by Robert D. Lynn Associates, illustrates the dual life of a major urban edifice. Inside, it houses a 24-bed surgical ICU, four 28-bed patient care units and ambulatory care facilities, which connect with existing hospital facilities on five different levels. Outside, its brick, cast stone and glass exterior, designed in association with Payette Associates of Boston, Massachusetts, respectfully converses with University architecture.

Kidspeace Child & Adolescent Psychiatric Hospital
Orefield, Pennsylvania

Left: Exterior
Below left: Patio/deck.
Below right:
Enclosed walkway
between facilities.
Opposite: Gymnasium.
Photography: Matt
Wargo.

Kidspeace Child & Adolescent Psychiatric Hospital, Orefield, Pennsylvania, offers a timely and affirmative look at a 116-bed, state-of-the-art psychiatric hospital for the young. At the heart of the sprawling 114,000-square foot, two-story structure, designed by Robert D. Lynn Associates, is an administrative and education building comprising therapy areas, classrooms, gymnasium, administrative and recreational areas as well as shared exhibit spaces. The children reside in dormitory-style residential clusters that house 24 patients each and include living rooms, game rooms, kitchen areas and supervised living units. Wherever they go within this friendly, colorful and non-threatening environment, patients, staff and visitors can find the care and support they need.

Fairfax Hospital
Women and Children's Center
Falls Church, Virginia

Serving a young, growing population is the strategy behind the new, 305,000-square foot Women and Children's Center at Fairfax Hospital, Falls Church, Virginia, designed by Robert D. Lynn Associates. Recognizing the power of a patient-focused environment to affect patient outcomes, the Hospital and the designers have created a friendly, non-institutional yet effective facility appointed in attractive, contemporary furnishings and bathed in indirect and natural light.

Throughout the 128 OB beds, 18 LDR rooms, 36 GYN beds, 48-bed pediatric unit, six-bed pediatric ICU, six-bed pediatric step-down unit, 44-bed NICU and ancillary support spaces to handle over 10,000 births a year, the new Center acknowledges the vital roles that patients, staff and visitors play in birth and healing.

Top: *Exterior.*
Above: *Physical thearpy reception and waiting room.*

Above right: *NICU waiting area.*
Right: *LDR room.*
Photography: *Kenneth M. Wyner.*

RDLA • Robert D. Lynn Associates

Christiana Hospital
Newark, Delaware

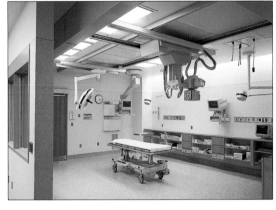

Left: *Exterior of new OB wing.*
Lower left: *Treatment room ED.*
Bottom: *Emergency medicine.*
Photography: *Tom Bernard.*

Both emergency medicine and obstetrics medicine have experienced considerable innovation in recent years, and the benefits are on display at Christiana Hospital, Newark, Delaware, which recently completed a 175,000-square foot expansion and 12,000-square foot renovation, designed by Robert D. Lynn Associates. Acute care, fast track and observation are now separated in the ED, which is equipped with radiographic, CT and ultrasound facilities as well as a direct link to the existing surgical suite. Having a separate drop-off point from the main hospital entrance, OB boasts 16 LDR rooms, three delivery rooms, eight high-risk rooms, all with advanced design and technology, and immediate access to the existing NICU. Whether the Hospital is treating an annual workload of 84,000 ED visits, 7,000 deliveries or other demands for health care services, it's in excellent condition.

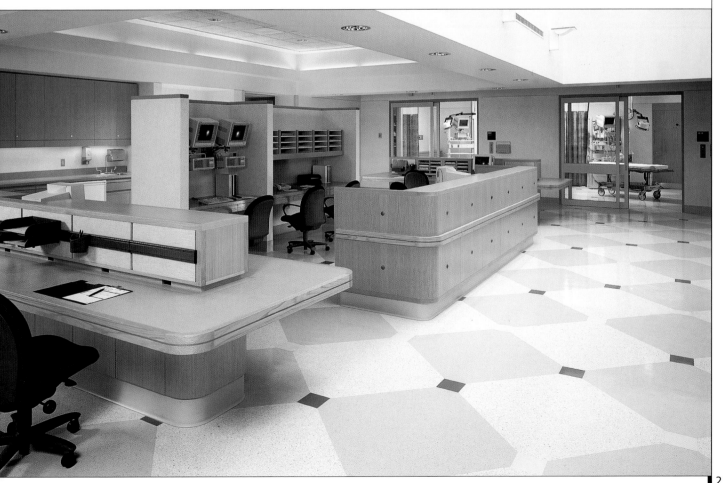

Bucks County Specialty Care Center
Children's Hospital of Philadelphia
New Britain Township, Pennsylvania

Left: *Entry vestibule.*
Below: *Exterior.*
Photography: *Matt Wargo.*

Today's popular community health centers are epitomized by the new, 42,600-square foot Bucks County Specialty Care Center, New Britain Township, Pennsylvania, designed by Robert D. Lynn Associates. Community-based pediatric care services such as radiology, audiology, physical and occupational therapy and phlebotomy are housed here, along with treatment areas for cardiology, neurology, opthamology, and ear, nose and throat. Facilities also include accommodations for reception, waiting, check-out, clerical support, conferences and staff activity. Useful as it already is, the Center will be more valued when the planned expansion of the existing ambulatory surgical center is constructed.

SmithGroup

SmithGroup
1825 Eye Street, NW
Suite 250
Washington, DC 20006
202.842.2100
202.974.4500 (Fax)
www.smithgroup.com

SmithGroup JJR
110 Miller Avenue
Ann Arbor
Michigan 48104
734.662.4457
734.662.7520 (Fax)

Ann Arbor
Chicago
Detroit
Los Angeles
Madison
Manila
Miami
Phoenix
Reston
San Francisco
Washington, DC

SmithGroup

Womack Army Medical Center
Fort Bragg, North Carolina

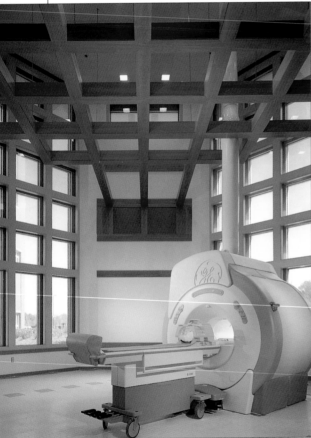

Top: Outpatient Building exterior.
Above left: Imaging center.
Above right: Dining room.
Right: Chapel.
Opposite: Outpatient entrance lobby.
Photography: Justin Maconochie/Hedrich Blessing.

For a 1.14 million-square-foot, three-story facility serving military personnel at North Carolina's Fort Bragg and Pope Air Base and logging 1 million outpatient visits annually, the new, replacement hospital for Womack Army Medical Center, designed by SmithGroup, feels unexpectedly intimate, humane and comfortable. The design of the Center's outpatient clinic, ancillary diagnostic/treatment building, 319-bed nursing tower, central circulation spine and freestanding central plant establishes interconnected elements whose systems function independently, resulting in optimal efficiency and flexibility. A significant aesthetic benefit of this approach is that the Center resembles a campus of buildings with landscaped courtyards rather than a megastructure. The highly articulated forms and materials in the architecture and interior design humanize its large, systems-driven form, and gracefully sites it on its 160 acres of woodland.

SmithGroup

**Thornton Hospital
University of California
San Diego
La Jolla, California**

No one likes the pain, isolation or disorientation of hospitalization, but losing control of our lives probably hurts the most. Accordingly, the University of California San Diego's new, 253,000-square-foot Thornton Hospital, La Jolla, has been designed by SmithGroup to alleviate the patient's sense of helplessness. A key component is the Patient Care Information System, which enters patient data directly into a bedside computer for immediate access by physicians, staff and patient. Another is the patient room, offering such features as monitors and medical instruments built into a console at the head of the bed, windows with lowered window sills for bedridden individuals, and a "light shelf" above each main window reflecting daylight deep inside. Thornton represents an auspicious start for the first facility on UC San Diego's new east campus. Its comfortable, efficient and non-institutional environment, developed with help from the hotel industry and backed by an array of integrated building systems, will make its projected growth from 120 to 400 beds an event patients can sincerely appreciate.

Above: Inner court.
Above left: Waiting room.
Left: Corridor to rotunda.
Right: Patient room.
Opposite: Atrium.
Photography: David Hewitt, Anne Garrison.

SmithGroup　　**Moser Cancer Center University of Virginia Health System Charlottesville, Virginia**

Are the stress and isolation of outpatient cancer treatment more bearable through design? The possibilities are showcased at the 7,000-square-foot Moser Cancer Center, Charlottesville, Virginia, designed for the University of Virginia Health System by SmithGroup. Treating patients outside the traditional boundaries of UVA's Health Sciences Center, the new facility and its linear accelerator surround patients in a less institutional and more residential setting. Here patients are encouraged to interact to lessen their anxiety and respond better to treatment through living room-like patient waiting areas that overlook healing garden courtyards. "It is truly a wonderful environment for patients and staff," says Dr. Jules Levine, associate vice president for health sciences at UVA. "Patients have told us that they appreciate the privacy, the courtyard gardens and the 'non-institutional,' non-threatening character of the building."

SmithGroup

Sutter Amador Hospital
Jackson, California

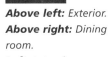
Above left: *Exterior.*
Above right: *Dining room.*
Left: *Intensive care unit.*
Lower left: *Waiting area.*
Photography: *Michael O'Callahan.*

Health services and community affairs form a unique partnership at Sutter Amador Hospital in Jackson, California. The 93,000-square-foot, 66-bed replacement hospital, designed by SmithGroup as design architect and Silva Strong Architects as architect of record, serves the rural population of Amador County in one of the area's few public buildings. As a result, a public meeting room is included on the first floor, and a sense of community pervades waiting areas through inviting interiors and generous views of the surrounding landscape. Shaker-style furniture, quilts by local artists, cherry wood cabinetry and other residential-like furnishings characterize the space—which incorporates acute and critical care nursing units, surgery, imaging, outpatient/urgent care center, clinical laboratory and emergency—projecting a warm, friendly atmosphere in a highly economical, efficient and technological facility. John Millsap, former facilities development director for Sutter Health System, calls Sutter Amador "the best hospital in the whole system."

SmithGroup   Mount Zion Outpatient Cancer Center, University of California San Francisco
San Francisco, California

Above left: *Outpatient lobby.*
Above right: *Waiting area.*
Top right: *Exterior.*
Photography: *Michael O'Callahan.*

It's impressive how a new entry can transform a hospital. With the addition of the 86,000-square foot Outpatient Cancer Center, designed by SmithGroup, Mount Zion Medical Center has created a new atrium that is linked to the existing main lobby, consolidating and enhancing the entrances to the outpatient and inpatient facilities. The new outpatient entry is a white-painted tubular steel and glass structure that is mirrored by the remodeled existing structure and new tubular steel and glass canopy at the inpatient entry/vehicular drop off.

Equally significant, of course, are the new accommodations for radiation oncology, breast care, infusion and other specialty clinics, helping the Center win the prestigious designation of National Institute of Health-Comprehensive Cancer Center.

The Stein-Cox Group

821 North Central Avenue
Phoenix
Arizona 85004
602.462.0966
602.462.9495 (Fax)
www.stein-cox.com
sally@stein-cox.com

The Stein-Cox Group

TMC Advanced Imaging
Palm Valley
Goodyear, Arizona

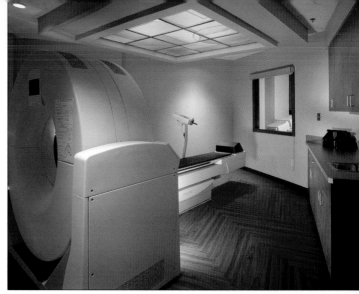

Patients in imaging centers can give many reasons why they would prefer their environments to feel home-like, as is the case at the new, 3,700-square foot TMC Advanced Imaging - Palm Valley in Goodyear, Arizona, designed by The Stein Cox Group. It could involve having to surrender street clothes, uncertainty about procedures, fear of the massive and impersonal imaging equipment, or physical discomfort from holding still against cold steel. In any event, the experience is highly stressful, a situation TMC directly addresses in its high-tech space. Aside from resolving such technical matters as shielding requirements, the designers have introduced comfort and interest through open floor plans, non-institutional lighting and Arts and Crafts-style furnishings that soften the impact of the facility's MRI, CT and ultrasound equipment. Patients coming here know that this imaging center is different—for the right reasons.

Opposite above:
Imaging room.
Opposite below:
Reception.
Below: Patient area.
Photography: Mark
Boisclair.

The Stein-Cox Group

Fresno Heart Hospital
Fresno, California

Right: Entrance court.
Below left: Site plan.
Below right: Overall façade.
Photography: Peter Dozal.

One of the compliments regularly heard about the new, 134,500-square foot Fresno Heart Hospital in Fresno, California, designed by The Stein-Cox Group, in association with Lew and Patnaude, is that it does not "look like or feel like" a hospital. It's a major priority to accomplish at the freestanding cardiac care hospital, which will provide cardiac care to a growing population with four cardiac cath labs, three operating rooms, a 16- bed cardiac day program, a 12-bed ICU, 48 private rooms, an outpatient cardiology program and a cardiac emergency department. The facility comprises a four-story patient tower connected by a bridge to a two- story building for operating rooms and cardiac cath labs. True to its mission, the hospital challenges health care norms through good wayfinding, patient rooms that face an adjacent park and mountain vistas, and can accommodate relatives or friends overnight. Friendly, residential-style furnishings and Internet connections are in all patient rooms. There's no need to "look like or feel like" a hospital here.

The Stein-Cox Group

Arizona Heart Hospital
Phoenix, Arizona

It's one thing to develop a major health care facility in just 14 months from site acquisition through design and construction, but to break new ground in patient care and staff efficiencies at the same time is a testament to the close collaboration between seasoned architects and an inspired health care client. This is indeed the story of the new, 140,000-square foot, 59-bed Arizona Heart Hospital, Phoenix, Arizona, designed by The Stein-Cox Group and HDR. The two-story structure, centered around a cath/surgical core with four cath labs and three open-heart rooms, is fully planned with a patient-focused care model to separate inpatients and outpatients, locate required patient services to reduce travel, and offer families convenient and private gathering areas that are modern and upbeat, setting an encouraging benchmark for similar institutions to come.

Right: *Entrance lobby and reception.*
Left: *Operating room.*
Opposite right: *Exterior.*
Photography: *Mark Boisclair.*

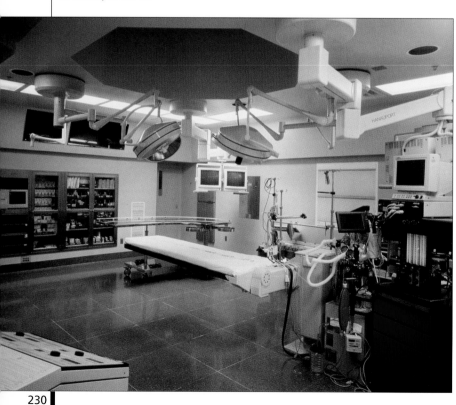

The Stein-Cox Group

Del E. Webb Memorial Hospital
Sun City West, Arizona

Health care administrators must project future facility needs knowing that such needs can never be precisely known. Splendid results are possible nevertheless, such as the 209,400-square foot expansion and 52,140-square foot remodel of Del E. Webb Memorial Hospital in Sun City West, Arizona, designed by The Stein-Cox Group and HKS. The project's main component, a new, full-service Women's Health Center, and various additions to existing departments should safely see the rapidly changing community to 2006 in attractive, state-of-the-art style.

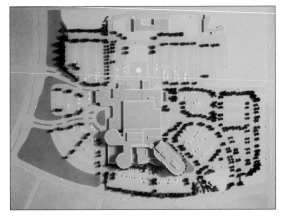

Above left: Exterior.
Above right: Site plan.
Left: Overview of site.
Photography: Steven Vaughan.

The Stichler Group

9655 Granite Ridge Drive
Suite 400
San Diego
California 92123
888.784.2453
858.569.3433 (Fax)
www.stichler.com
info@stichler.com

The Stichler Group

The Stichler Group

Lawrence J. Ellison Ambulatory Care Center
University of California, Davis
Sacramento, California

Being large, yet conveying a feeling of small, is not an easy feat for a 377,000-square foot, four-level health care complex covering more than a city block. Nevertheless, the image of a highly approachable and patient-friendly institution is strongly projected by the Lawrence J. Ellison Ambulatory Care Center at University of California, Davis, designed by The Stichler Group. Given the facility's mission, it could not have enclosed less than the imposing floor area that it shelters. The Center is one of the largest ambulatory care centers in the nation, encompassing all of UC Davis Medical Center's primary care and multi-specialty clinics, along with a full spectrum of pharmacy, laboratory, physical therapy, radiology and other diagnostic services. Yet the building's mission goes beyond the delivery of healthcare services as a component of UC Davis College of Medicine by providing academic offices and classrooms. To keep the resulting structure from imposing its bulk on the site, the program has been allocated among numerous moderately scaled volumes and anchored by a pedestrian mall extending the length of the complex that aids wayfinding with lush landscaping, an ambulatory course for physical therapy patients and outdoor dining and seating areas. Here, bigger can be better.

Opposite: Outdoor
dining in pedestrian mall.
Left: Outpatient imaging
waiting area.
Right: Outpatient
entrance/information
area/reception.
Above: Outpatient
entrance.
Photography: Brett
Drury.

The Stichler Group

Mary Birch Hospital for Women
San Diego, California

Women's inpatient and outpatient needs are the sole mission of the 197,000-square foot Mary Birch Hospital for Women, San Diego, California, designed by The Stichler Group. Sandwiched on a tight site between two other operating hospital structures, the new hospital serves as a pedestrian link between parking structures and adjacent Sharp Memorial Hospital, even as it establishes its own, for-women-only identity. To create an environment of spaciousness and light for patients, the hospital incorporates three atriums, landscaped primarily with palms and bamboo, as part of an overall interior design scheme that is informal, relaxed and outdoors-oriented. Another sensitive response to the hospital's clientele is the separation of admissions areas for women requir-ing prenatal care, who are frequently not ill in any way, from those coming in for other types of services. Among the numerous facilities offered are 108 adult beds, 61 NICU beds with a parent living unit, 22 LDRP units and a discharge area, a center for psychosocial assessment and intervention, health resource library, plus a variety of diagnostic and therapy facilities. The message of the overall design is unmistakable: Women will find a welcoming place at Mary Birch Hospital.

Above: Entry exterior.
Below left: Typical LDR room.
Below right: Information desk.
Opposite: Atrium.
Photography: Brett Drury.

236

The Stichler Group

Kaiser Permanente Otay Mesa Outpatient Medical Center
San Diego, California

Can a "one-stop shopping" facility for comprehensive outpatient services simultaneously offer convenience for patients and economies for their health maintenance organization? This was the challenge confronted by Kaiser Permanente's 257,000-square foot Otay Mesa Outpatient Medical Center in San Diego, California, designed by The Stichler Group. The complex was built in three phases. The first phase, completed less than two years from the outset of programming, included primary care services, OB/GYN and pediatrics as well as radiology and eye services departments. The second and third phases, finished the following year, added internal medicine, dermatology, urology, neurology, orthopedics, general surgery, eye and neck surgery, and a Wellness Center of eight classrooms and treatment rooms to engage patients in a holistic view of their health. For the added convenience of patients, the facility has extensive surface parking areas which lead to several entry courtyards and lobbies that converge on a central wayfinding point, a half-acre interior courtyard that quickly directs them to the care they seek.

Right: *Lobby.*
Below right: *Clinic check-in lobby.*
Bottom: *Exterior.*
Opposite: *Courtyard.*
Photography: *John Durante.*

The Stichler Group

A.B. and Jessie Polinsky Children's Center
San Diego, California

Right: Typical cottage.
Below left: Cottage kitchen.
Below right: Gymnasium.
Bottom right: Reception lobby.
Photography: John Durrant.

Whatever the escalating need for child protective and social services says about contemporary society, the new, 90,000-square foot A.B. and Jessie Polinsky Children's Center in San Diego, California, designed by The Stichler Group, provides a vital service for 130 children ranging from newborns to 18 years in age. Because the facility's six residential cottages and adjacent school, library, gym, and outdoor pool reside in an industrial and commercial area, they focus inward on their landscaped site. Yet the Center is secure without being confined, using plantings and architecture rather than fences to draw the children into a loving embrace.

Swanke Hayden Connell Architects
Taylor Clark Healthcare Group

25 Christopher Street
London
England EC2A 2BS
44171.454.8200
44171.454.8400 (Fax)

295 Lafayette Street
New York
New York 10012
212.226.9696
212.219.0059 (Fax)

1030, 15th Street, NW
Suite 1000
Washington, DC 20005
202.789.1200
202.789.1432 (Fax)

www.shca.com

First Union Financial Center
200 South Biscayne Boulevard
Suite 970
Miami
Florida 33131.2300
305.536.8600
305.536.8610 (Fax)

84 West Park Place
Stamford
Connecticut 06901
203.348.9696
203.348.9914 (Fax)

Kore Sehitleri Cad.
No. 34/2 Deniz Is Hani
80300 Zincirlikuyu
Istanbul
Türkiye
90.212.275.4590
90.212.275.3780 (Fax)

17 Rue Campagne Premiére
75014 Paris
France
33.1 56 54 14 90
33.1 56 54 14 94 (Fax)

Swanke Hayden Connell
Taylor Clark Healthcare Group

New York Hospital Queens
Flushing, New York

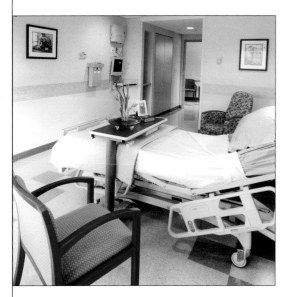

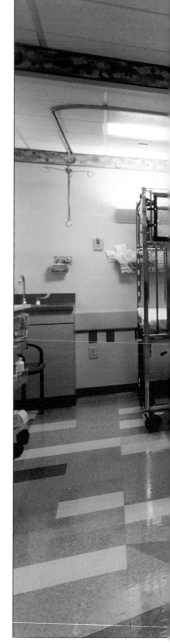

Upper left: Patient room in LDR unit.
Below left: NICU Unit.
Below right: Procedure Room.
Photography: Stan Ries.

Proof of the burgeoning population in New York City's Borough of Queens is the daily traffic at New York Hospital Medical Center of Queens in Flushing. To meet rising demand for services for mothers and children, the Hospital recently added a new, 75,000-square foot, three-story East Pavilion, designed by Swanke Hayden Connell Architects. Its 30 OB nursing units, 32 bassinet well baby nursery, nine LDR beds, three c-section rooms, five recovery beds and a 14 incubator NICU unit collectively establish a non-institutional setting that is popular with the area's families, who come from all over the world. Among the special features they appreciate are a patient/medical information system with a flat screen beside every patient bed, and a Baby-on-the-Net service that lets relatives and friends worldwide see the newborns a few hours after birth. Equally innovative is the new, first floor emergency department that includes a designated pediatric emergency area. Infused with color, this dedicated area is demonstrative of the increasing need healthcare facilities have for specialized areas, like ones that cater to women and children, in uplifting and vibrant atmospheres.

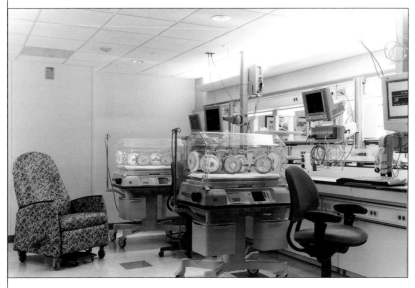

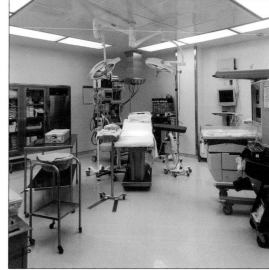

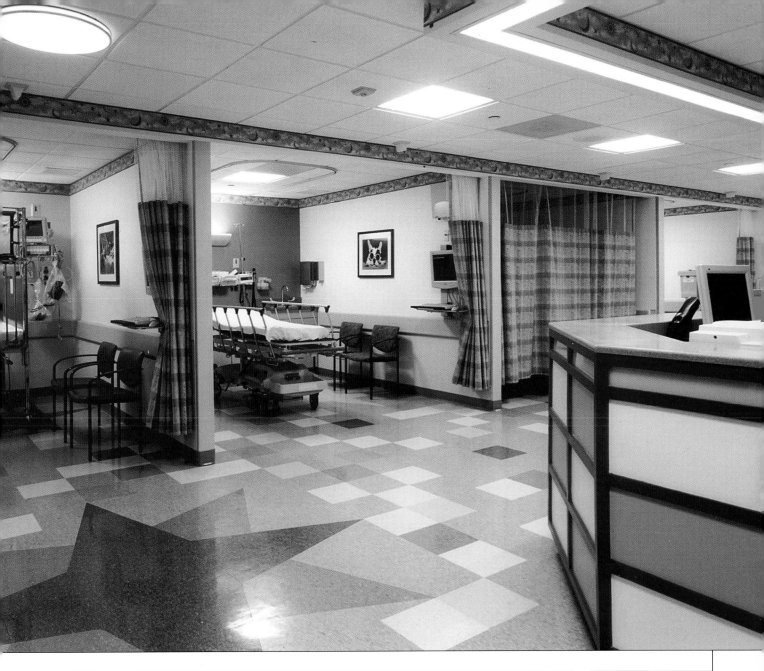

Swanke Hayden Connell
Taylor Clark Healthcare Group

Melrose Wakefield Hospital
Special Care Nursery, Women &
Children Services
Melrose, Massachusetts

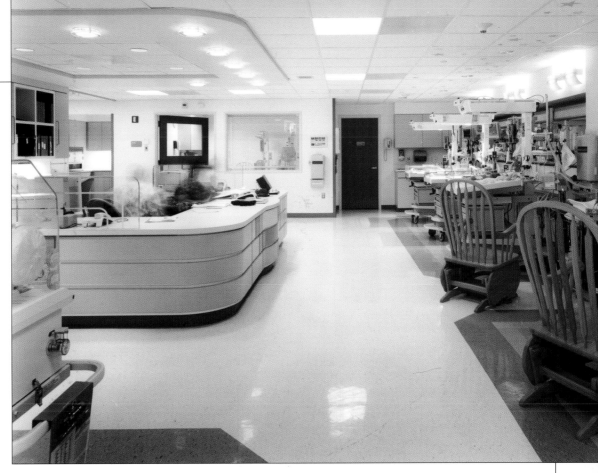

Parents can expect better care for newborns at Melrose Wakefield Hospital in Melrose, Massachusetts, 20 miles north of Boston, because Hallmark Health Systems and Swanke Hayden Connell Architects have developed a new and wonderfully supportive Special Care Nursery. The 4,500-square foot, 4th-floor facility not only provides a hygienic, safe, state-of-the-art environment for newborns with securely zoned circulation and a dedicated elevator to the 2nd-floor LDRP and C-section units, it sustains a setting that is comforting to users and visitors alike. Its nine infant stations (expandable to 13), nurses station, isolation room and ancillary facilities make such exemplary use of millwork, wallcoverings, carpet and vinyl flooring, hollow-metal and steel, specialty art and glass that Massachusetts Department of Public Health officials have declared that it is the most carefully designed and detail-oriented space of its kind in the state.

Swanke Hayden Connell
Taylor Clark Healthcare Group

Payne Whitney Clinic
New York Presbyterian Hospital
New York, New York

Remodeling a hospital is like excavating an archeological site—anything you touch affects everything around it. Consider the recent redesign and relocation of the 50,000-square foot Payne Whitney Clinic at Manhattan's New York Presbyterian Hospital, which Swanke Hayden Connell Architects served as planner and designer. Besides working around existing facilities, structural members and building systems, the Clinic imposed conditions that made its psychiatric day hospital, pediatric psychiatric facility, outpatient facility and research facilities for functional neuroimaging as distinctive as they are handsome. The Oskar Diethelm Library, a treasury of 15th-19th-century psychiatric literature, required a complex fire prevention system to let it perform as a natural dividing line between the psychiatric educational division and the chairman and visiting doctors' suites. A departmental staircase penetrated three floors by navigating through a forest of beams and columns. Original artifacts from the Clinic's 1932 building were incorporated at various focal points on the main level for all entering patients to see. The success of this transplant is reflected in abundant praise from Dr. Jack Barchas, psychiatrist-in-chief, and his colleagues.

Above: Reception and waiting room.
Opposite, left: Departmental staircase.
Opposite, right: Library entrance.
Right: Lecture hall.
Photography: Walter Dufresne.

Swanke Hayden Connell
Taylor Clark Healthcare Group

Vassar Brothers Hospital
Poughkeepsie, New York

With the opening of its new, glass-enclosed reception lobby, three-story west wing, and pedestrian walkway linking the lobby to the new parking garage, Vassar Brothers Hospital has dramatically enhanced its service to the historic Hudson Valley community of Poughkeepsie, New York. The existing structure was modified to meet new requirements and new construction was added over seven years to complete a $70-million consolidation of similar departments and creation of two new programs involving cardiothoracic surgery and labor, delivery, recovery and postpartum (LDRP) units. Given the need to maintain ongoing services, acknowledge changing circumstances, monitor schedules and costs, and update medical equipment and technology during this lengthy interval, the architects stayed in close, continuous collaboration with the Hospital. For an institution that pledges, "The care they need close to home," the wait has been amply rewarded with a handsome and effective facility.

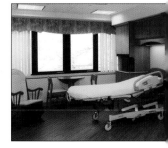

Top left: Exterior.
Left: Reception lobby.
Above: Patient room in LDRP unit.
Photography: Bernstein Associates.

Taylor & Associates Architects

2220 North University Drive
Newport Beach
California 92660
949.574.1325
949.574.1338 (Fax)
www.taa1.com
info@taa1.com

Taylor & Associates Architects

Taylor & Associates Architects

Hoag Breast Care and Imaging Center
Hoag Memorial Hospital Presbyterian
Newport Beach, California

To remodel an existing facility for mammography, imaging, diagnostic services, and consultation to resemble a "sophisticated spa," is especially daunting when the facility is underground. That was the reality facing the Hoag Breast Care and Imaging Center, in the basement of a medical office building, when Taylor & Associates Architects confronted the 8,435-square foot space. The remodeled Center addresses patients' concerns even as it overcomes physical limitations. A corridor wall has been replaced by a concealed fire partition, for example, to create a spacious waiting room visible to patients stepping off the elevator. Staggered ceiling planes are indirectly illuminated to simulate daylight. Steel, limestone, textured glass, pear wood, paper-like wallcoverings and comfortable furniture in soft fabrics collectively make a rich interior.

Left: *Sub-waiting area.*
Photography: *Assassi Productions.*

Above: Lobby and
reception area.
Left: Dressing room.
Below: Waiting room.

MemorialCare Breast Center at Anaheim Memorial Medical Center Anaheim, California

Above: *Gowned waiting area.*
Right: *Patient check out.*
Opposite: *Waiting and reception.*
Photography: *Assassi Productions.*

Does it make sense to appoint a new, state-of-the-art women's comprehensive breast care center in traditional, residential-style furnishings that are often fragile and hard to maintain? The determination of Anaheim Memorial Medical Center in Anaheim, California to develop a new, 3,495-square foot, MemorialCare Breast Center in a contemporary style encouraged Taylor & Associates Architects to carefully explore how the aggressive forms of today's interior architecture could genuinely serve feminine needs. The Center's blend of crisp, orthogonal partitions and such cool, contemporary materials as metal and glass with pastel colors, indirect lighting and curvilinear ceilings has so altered what was once the executive offices that the number of women patients has increased by 30 percent.

Taylor & Associates Architects   **Hoag Hospital East Tower**
Women's Pavilion
Newport Beach, California

Hoag Hospital's East Tower, the Women's Pavilion, is admittedly large at 320,035 square feet, with seven floors above grade, a basement and a rooftop mechanical floor. However, the sophisticated design by Taylor & Associates Architects will make a patient's experience much more intimate. Because of its dedication to patients' needs, there are such facilities as "rooming in" postpartum patient rooms, where newborns stay with their mothers instead of the nursery, and daybeds are provided for fathers' overnight use.

Taylor & Associates Architects

Kaiser Permanente Medical Office Buildings Yorba Linda, Santa Ana and East Los Angeles, California

Kaiser Permanente has enjoyed a reputation over the years as a savvy developer of health care facilities, and three Kaiser Permanente Medical Office Buildings designed by Taylor & Associates Architects in Yorba Linda, Santa Ana and East Los Angeles strongly reaffirm that reputation. The buildings, varying in size from 50,000 square feet in Yorba Linda and East Los Angeles to 80,000 square feet in Santa Ana (in two phases) provide outpatient care that may include a nurse clinic, vision services, laboratory, radiology, pharmacy, family practice, pediatric practice, OB/GYN practice and physical therapy. The trio adhere to Kaiser Permanente area planning standards internally, but are enclosed in handsome architectural envelopes that have been designed to respect and enhance the unique aesthetic qualities of the surrounding communities.

Upper left: Yorba Linda exterior.
Upper right: Santa Ana exterior.
Left: East Los Angeles exterior.

Photography: Ronald Moore (upper left); Taylor & Associates Architects (upper right). **Illustration:** Taylor & Associates Architects.

Taylor & Associates Architects

The New White Memorial
White Memorial Medical Center-Adventist Health
Los Angeles, California

Residents East of downtown Los Angeles can look forward to the New White Memorial Medical Center, a 450,000-square foot replacement and remodeled hospital designed by Taylor & Associates Architects. This ambitious facility, encompassing an emergency department, surgery, imaging, labor and delivery, neonatal intensive care unit, intensive care unit and medical/ surgical unit, will respond directly to the community's medical needs and Latino roots. When completed in 2006, the new acute care hospital will maximize the reuse of two existing acute care buildings by being inserted between them to establish a functioning health care campus. The exterior draws its inspiration from the forms and materials of the California colonial style, firmly tying the new institution to the people it will serve.

Tsoi/Kobus & Associates

One Brattle Square
P.O. Box 9114
Cambridge
Massachusetts 02238
617.491.3067
617.864.0265 (Fax)
www.tka-architects.com

Tsoi/Kobus & Associates

Brigham and Women's Hospital
Boston, Massachusetts

Left: *Exterior.*
Below left: *LDR suite.*
Below right:
Postpartum corridor.
Opposite: *Lobby.*
Photography: *Steve Rosenthal.*

The culmination of over 10 years of strategic planning, programming and facilities master planning at Boston's Brigham and Women's Hospital by Tsoi/Kobus & Associates, the 265,000-square foot, 12-story Center for Women and Newborns (CWN) responds to a surge in demand for obstetrical services. The new facility consolidates previously scattered services for women in a single facility that houses a 24-bed labor/delivery/recovery suite with three high-risk obstetrics rooms and four cesarean section operating rooms, a 46-bed newborn intensive care unit with five family rooms and a solarium lounge, a 120-bed postpartum suite, various OB/GYN and women's health services, and the world's first interventional iMR suite. Designed to offer the most compre-

hensive continuum of women's medical services in the country, CWN focuses on strengthening the family unit in a facility that is both technologically state-of-the-art and warm and inviting. Patients and visitors must enter CWN through "The Pike," Brigham and Women's primary circulation spine, but the lobby's striking "front porch" image quickly assures them about the high quality, family focused health care they will find here.

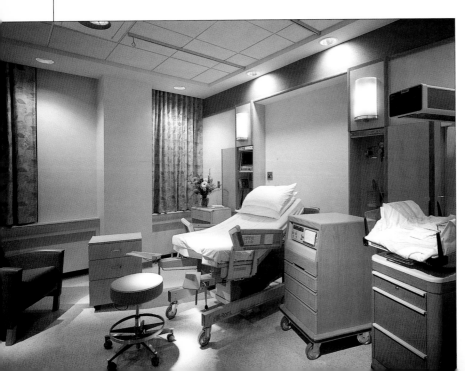

To maintain its leadership in women's health care, Pittsburgh's Magee-Womens Hospital is expanding its focus beyond a woman's reproductive years to provide a continuum of care throughout her life. Since 1992, Tsoi/Kobus & Associates has served Magee in developing and implementing a master plan to support this mission. The construction of a 369,000-square foot ambulatory care center, Womancare Oakland, inaugurates the first phase of the master plan. It bestows a forward-looking and unified appearance to an aging campus lacking in cohesion, achieves operational efficiencies through the centralization of key diagnostic and support functions on the lower levels, groups

medical office suites around the multi-level lobby to simplify patient access and orientation on upper levels, and surrounds everything in an interior environment of wood accents and abundant daylight. "Tsoi/Kobus & Associates is a firm that knows the business of architecture," says Irma Goertzen, president and CEO of Magee. "Beyond that, they have demonstrated a solid understanding of our business—women's health—and the broader spectrum of health care."

Left: Exterior.
Above: *Birthing Center reception.*
Below left: *Imaging facility.*
Below right: *Auditorium.*

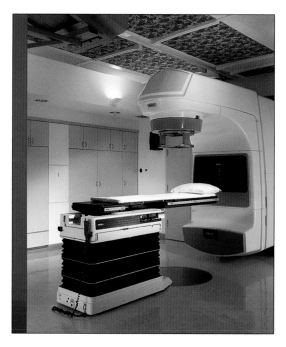

Tsoi/Kobus & Associates

University of Chicago Hospitals
Chicago, Illinois

Below: *Reception.*
Photography:
Scott McDonald/Hedrich Blessing.

You can discern the University of Chicago's continuing devotion to collegiate Gothic architecture on the exterior of the new 520,000-square foot, six-story Duchossois Center for Advanced Medicine (DCAM), which Tsoi/Kobus & Associates served as design architect in association with HLM Design, prime architect. The interior of the building is another story, however. Its mission is to improve and expand the ambulatory, diagnostic, treatment and research facilities of the University of Chicago Hospitals and University Pritzker School

of Medcine. As the Hospitals' first step in a long-term transition to ambulatory services and patient-focused care, DCAM serves chiefly outpatients in the ambulatory suites to the west of a four-story atrium, though the diagnostic and treatment wing to the east also serves inpatients. Among its accommodations are 250 examination rooms, 62 rooms for outpatient procedures (including three CT and two MRI scanners), facilities for nuclear medicine, eight outpatient surgery suites and four linear accelerators for radiation therapy.

Expansive, uninterrupted lower floors let large departments arrange themselves efficiently, while upper floors house clinical modules that let several subspecialties share practice space. The structural logic suits the Windy City fine, as do such finishing touches as the concessions and public activities that bring vitality to the atrium.

Above: Four-story atrium.
Right: Exterior.

Tsoi/Kobus & Associates

Massachusetts General Hospital
Northeast Proton Therapy Center
Boston, Massachusetts

Based on cyclotron technology developed at Harvard in the 1930s, the 44,900-square foot, three-level Northeast Proton Therapy Center in Boston, designed by Tsoi/Kobus & Associates, is one of the first such facilities in the world. The building posed such challenges as accommodating an exacting technology on a constricted site, creating a safe and welcoming environment for patients, and providing flexibility for the installation of a third treatment room and a future, 12-story addition and second-level bridge. Its environment is inescapably technical, with two above-grade levels housing an entry, administration, support and mechanical functions, and one below-grade level containing treatment areas whose 6-foot thick concrete walls shield radiation. Yet the exterior, featuring a dignified rotunda, and the interior, a sunny environment of bright colors and graceful forms, are an eloquent affirmation of life.

Above left: *Stairway to treatment areas.*
Above right: *Exterior.*
Photography: *Steve Rosenthal.*

264

URS

3950 Sparks Drive, S.E.
Grand Rapids
Michigan 49546
616.574.8500   Cleveland
616.574.8542 (Fax)   Denver
                      Indianapolis
277 West Nationwide Blvd.   New York
Columbus   Paramus
Ohio 43215   San Francisco
614.464.4500   Seattle
614.464.0588 (Fax)   Tampa
                      Toronto
www.urscorp.com   Washington, DC

Marietta Memorial Hospital
Outpatient Surgery Center
Marietta, Ohio

Above: Operating
rooms.
Right: Lobby/reception
area.
Far right: Pre- and post-
operative patient rooms.
Photography: Kirk
Fisher/Imagemakers
Photographic, Inc.

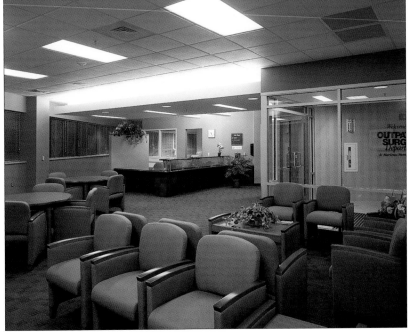

Being hospitalized for surgery takes on a new meaning at the new, 25,000-square foot Outpatient Surgery Center of Marietta Memorial Hospita. First, a central reception staff member welcomes you into a large waiting area that includes a separate children's play area, public restrooms, sit-down telephone area and refreshment center. Everything else is equally patient-friendly and efficient. Ten pre- and post-operative single patient rooms are located beyond the waiting area in a U-shape around the central nurses station, which is served by the same central service core that supports the operating area. Close by are separate consultation rooms, generous staff area and separate staff entrance. Patients can take care of everything here, from personal and medical information to being discharged. Surrounded by wood-accented public areas, comfortable furnishings, generous windows and indirect lighting, the staff and public laud the new facility designed by URS.

URS

Renucci Hospitality House
Spectrum Health
Grand Rapids, Michigan

Healthcare professionals have long realized the important therapeutic role that families and friends play in treating acutely ill patients. The Renucci Hospitality House, a new, 31,866 square foot, five-story, 36-room lodging, offers support to the families and friends of patients at the adjacent Spectrum Health campus. Spectrum Health provides the only Level 1 trauma center, regional burn center, and children's hospital in western Michigan. Many of Renucci House's guests are the families of patients in pediatric intensive care and neonatal intensive care. Other guests have patients in oncology, adult critical and adult surgical care. Developed on a tight urban site, Renucci House provides four floors of guest rooms and a ground floor with a reception lobby and control desk. The ground floor common areas provide a family room, children's room, library, dining rooms and gardens. All these amenities provide warmth, comfort and care to Renucci House's guests, as they provide care to others.

Above: Exterior.
Below: Guest room.
Bottom: Suite for bone marrow patient.

URS

Pentagon Tri-Service Ambulatory Care Clinic
Arlington, Virginia

The new 60,000 square foot Ambulatory Care Clinic in the United States Pentagon is a welcome addition to the Department of Defense's largest facility. Designed by URS as a single point of service, the clinic provides scheduled appointments, walk-ins and emergency medical treatment to the 25,000 military and civilian personnel assigned to the Pentagon. The clinic also provides these services to several thousand dependents and retired personnel, as well as any of the pentagon's daily visitors who might need emergency medical treatment. The new facility, completed after numerous phased construction challenges, occupies a former underground parking area below the historic River Terrace and above the new central data processing center. With the clinic's completion, the Pentagon now offers an additional level of security to its thousands of employees.

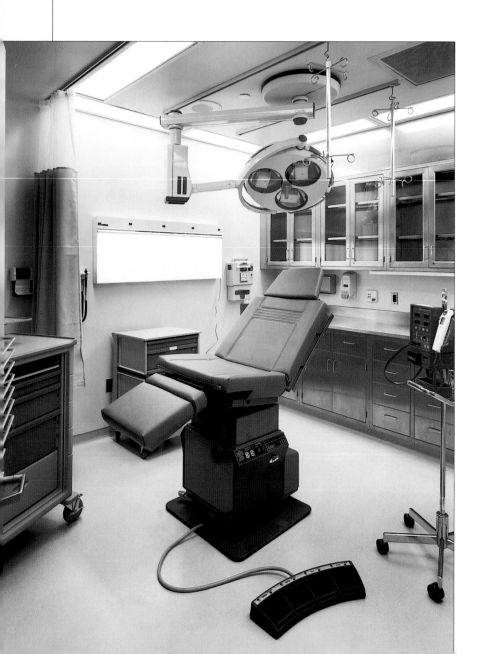

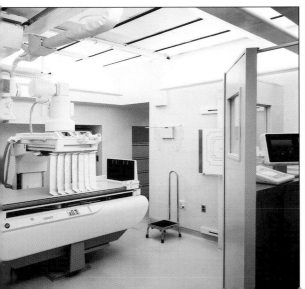

Indiana Surgery Center
Noblesville, Indiana

Facilities such as the new, 30,000-square foot Indiana Surgery Center that was designed by URS, shows how health care facilities large and small are being transformed by new concepts. Since most patients arrive and depart on the same day, concern for their comfort has produced an attractive and patient-friendly environment that maximizes efficiency and minimizes cross traffic. Upon registering, for example, patients and their families are escorted to one of 15 private patient rooms to prepare for their procedure. After they leave one of four operating rooms, patients proceed to the phase 1 recovery room before returning to their patient rooms to be reunited with their families. The center, which also includes support and administrative spaces, a waiting room with booths for snacking, play and computer use, a lounge for patients' families, and individual physicians' offices, is not a hospital--and needn't be.

Top: Patient visitor entry/drop-off.
Left: Nursing/staff work station.
Above: Lobby/reception area.
Photography: Greg Murphey.

Watkins Hamilton Ross Architects

20 Greenway Plaza
Suite 450
Houston
Texas 77046
713.665.5665
713.665.6213 (Fax)
www.whrarchitects.com

Watkins Hamilton Ross Architects

Dr. Bressler's Office
Houston, Texas

Being a specialist in plastic surgery of the face and neck, Dr. Bressler wanted his new, 2,958-square foot office in Houston, Texas, to be flawless in its own way. Instructing Watkins Hamilton Ross Architects to create a seamless flow between his marketing and his office, he literally handed over his business card and added, "Design a space like this." Careful planning ensured that patients do indeed regard the office as a sophisticated and pleasurable experience. Among the telling details in the floor plan are consultation/examination room suites that avoid the need to move patients from room to room, a sub-waiting area for private waiting and discreet exiting after a procedure, and private offices that provide the staff a relaxed and productive atmosphere. A multi-level ceiling, residential-style furniture, understated color palette, artwork, noninstitutional accessories and fresh flowers complete the unblemished visual image.

Above: Nurse station.
Right: Consultation/ examination room.
Opposite: View to waiting room.
Photography: Jud Haggard.

274

**Watkins Hamilton Ross
Architects**

**Morristown Memorial Hospital
Carol G. Simon Cancer Center
Morristown, New Jersey**

Above: Lobby.
Right: Registration
area with conference
room.
Below right: Exterior.
Photography:
Rex Spencer.

While the new Carol G. Simon Cancer Center at Morristown Memorial Hospital in Morristown, New Jersey, is noteworthy for many reasons, some are more conspicuous than others. The 82,000-square foot, three-story, above- and below-grade structure, designed by Watkins Hamilton Ross Architects, is one of only two U.S. cancer centers offering radiation therapy "intensity modulation" and the first providing a combined CT/linear accelerator vault within a facility comprising radiation oncology, medical oncology, women's center, private practice oncology/hematology clinic and such amenities as a patient resource center, skylights, water wall, meditation room and healing gardens. What patients may not realize is that combining the Center with a 35,000-square foot, six-operating room expansion of the surgery department made both projects sufficiently cost-effective to develop simultaneously. The resulting building, dramatically illuminated and warmly inviting, extends a unique welcome to patients and families who could not appreciate it more.

Watkins Hamilton Ross Architects

Memorial Hermann Hospital Pavilion
The Texas Medical Center
Houston, Texas

State-of-the-art medicine goes hand in hand with the heritage of a 1923 hospital building in the newly completed, 730,000-square foot, 14-level Memorial Hermann Hospital Pavilion at Houston's Texas Medical Center. The latest addition to a major teaching hospital, designed by Watkins Hamilton Ross Architects, encompasses a Children's Hospital, America's largest LDRP program, emergency center and trauma center. Outside, the Pavilion reflects the older building's Mediterranean style. Inside, patients, families and staff enjoy the convenience, comfort and technology of contemporary health care. For example, the 150-bed Children's Hospital shares services with the existing Hospital while offering such fresh concepts as a "town park," where children and parents can play and social-

Above: "Town park" in Children's Hospital.
Right: Nurses station in Children's Hospital.
Far right: Pavilion seen against 1923 building.
Opposite: Atrium lobby.
Photography: Jud Haggard (right and above), Larry Pearlstone (opposite).

Above left: *Patient room in Children's Hospital.*
Above right: *Pediatric emergency waiting room.*

Left: *Corridor in Children's Hospital.*
Above: *Nurses station in emergency center.*

ize, and family-friendly patient rooms grouped into six-bed "neighborhood" units. By embracing the single-room maternity concept, the LDRP program lets mothers stay in their rooms from the onset of labor through post-partum stay, eliminating risky transfers. And the emergency center features a separate pediatric emergency area that serves the needs of the Children's Hospital. Everything works so smoothly in the Pavilion that an attending physician recently told National Public Radio, "Everything is so quiet here, you can even hear the babies growing."

Be safe.

from head

to underfoot

For over fifty years, Altro has helped prevent slips and falls with our high performance sheet vinyl safety flooring.

Altro's wide range means we have a solution to meet all your flooring needs – for healthcare, hospitality, education, retail applications...and more.

In North America, slip and fall accidents are a billion dollar problem. Prevention is the best solution.

Protect yourself, your patients and your staff. Contact us about building safety into your floors.

Be safe.
Check before you spec.

ALTRO

AND WALLING

HIGH PERFORMANCE FLOORING

Armstrong offers you a wide range of flooring

products designed especially to meet the diverse

needs of hospitals and other health care facilities.

Dependable. Versatile. And performs well under stress. Not unlike an Armstrong floor.

Like Medintech, our most durable floor that

withstands the heavy load of operating room

equipment. Or Timberline, a natural wood look

in high-performance vinyl that provides a warm

environment in birthing suites. And Possibilities,

a superior stain-resistant floor that's great for

medical labs because it's so easy to clean. Our

floors also come in an array of warm, comforting

colors and vivid accents to make public areas

less institutional and more inviting. To find out

more, call 1-877-ARMSTRONG or visit us at

www.armstrong.com. For floors that perform

to the most exacting standards there are. Yours.

By Roger Yee

To Your Health

Can design transform health care facilities into extraordinary places to get well and stay well?

Watch the facial expressions of hospital patients if you suggest that they're actually staying in a guest house. Guest house is the meaning of the Latin word, hospitalis, that provided the name for today's institution. Hospitals first appeared in the Western world at the start of the Christian era to shelter sick or weary travelers and persons too poor or ill to be treated at home, yet their dirty, crowded and dark environments were anything but hospitable. Ironically, while health care management struggles to make the delivery of services and medication more cost-effective, and medical science and technology advance our ability to fight illness in new and often astonishing ways, the hospital is coming closer to its roots as a guest house in the best sense of the term. The health care industry is learning how to focus on satisfying the patient as a means of achieving market share and financial stability. Consequently, he or she is being treated more and more like a guest in a house or hotel.

Another case of better late than never? For centuries, health care design has reflected the procedures, equipment and opinions of health care providers, a logical precedent

*H*ospitals first appeared in the Western world at the start of the Christian era to shelter sick or weary travelers and persons too poor or ill to be treated at home, yet their dirty, crowded and dark environments were anything but hospitable.

even contemporary patients are unlikely to question. After all, who wants to interfere with the doctors, nurses and other personnel who are the most visible representatives of a highly successful institution when it comes time to build?

However, the direction of health care design is shifting perceptibly as research illuminates a previously neglected factor in combating sickness—the patient's emotional well-being. Psychoneuroimmunology, the study of the role that emotions play in the pathogenesis of physical diseases associated with immunological dysfunctions, has emerged as a promising field of inquiry with profound implications for design. If the patient's emotional condition influences the progress of his or her disease, mainly through increased or decreased stress and its consequences for the body, then the health care environment stands out as an important source of emotional stress or tranquillity that can be deliberately manipulated to help the patient.

In effect, architects and interior designers can actively contribute to improved patient outcomes by designing buildings and interiors of buildings to reduce the stress of

KI healthcare solutions. Comfort, quality, and function.

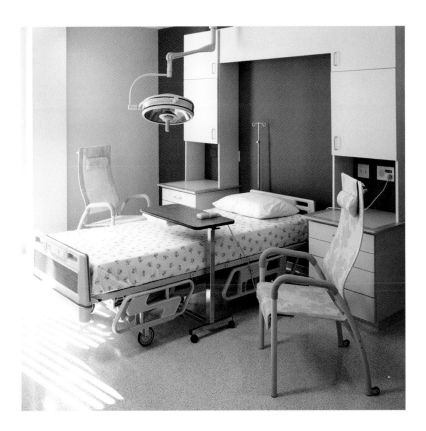

Whether helping hospital staff work better, patients heal faster, or family members rest easier, KI leads the way with award winning healthcare furniture solutions. The KI family of companies — ADD™, AGI™, Period™, Spacesaver,® and Pallas® — offer truly unique solutions for patient room and lobby/waiting room seating, administrative office furniture, site furnishings, high-density healthcare supply storage, and textiles that are hygienic, washable, and breathable. We'll improve the quality of life at your facility! KI...your source for innovative healthcare solutions!

Call 1-800-424-2432. Or visit www.ki.com.

KI | **WORKING FOR YOU**

treatment. By studying how a patient will respond to the spaces he or she encounters in the course of a stay that may last less than a day or more than several weeks, a designer can create a physical setting that directly addresses such emotional stresses as disorientation, isolation, fear, pain and powerlessness that patients commonly experience. But the process of designing a health care facility remains as much an art as it is a science, despite the conspicuously scientific context.

The reason is telling. Science simply does not know enough about how people experience space to instruct architects and interior designers about what works and why. As noted by respected interior designer and health care design consultant Jain Malkin in her comprehensive study, *Hospital Interior Architecture* (1992), "The principal hallmarks of scientific experimentation are that studies can be replicated and that variables can be controlled. Such experimentation is very difficult with architectural research." So the professional designer approaches the problem in his or her own way, blending design theory, scientific findings, empirical observations and interviews with building occupants—in this case, health care professionals, patients and their families—plus a healthy dose of artistic imagination.

Health care facility planning: How do you begin what will never be unfinished?

Focusing on patient needs thus becomes one of the leading concerns in the pro-

gramming, planning and design of a new health care facility, joining a host of other contemporary concerns. At the earliest stages of development, health care planners and designers have routinely acknowledged such prevailing conditions as the current and projected needs of the patient populations to be served, the capabilities of the staff and other institutions in the region, and the applicable building codes and health care regulations in the community. Today, the emotional stresses likely to confront staff, patients, their families and friends are added to the list.

The best-laid plans cannot prevent the mission of a major medical facility from changing over its 30- to 60-year life span. As for the patients, who knows what kind of health insurance coverage will be available to Americans in five or 10 years?

If young families are flocking to the surrounding area, for example, a new birthing center or children's hospital might soon be besieged by patients. Similarly, an aging Baby Boomer population is likely to seek extensive services related to aging, such as a sophisticated imaging center or cardio-vascular clinic. These current and projected demands would not necessarily be supplied by the new facility.

What's happened to the all-encompassing general hospital of the early postwar years, dramatized by such popular television shows as Medic, Dr. Kildare and Marcus Welby, M.D.? Since the 1970s, it has taken its place as part of a regional or community-wide health care system that rationalizes the distribution of basic and specialized services, staff and equipment to optimize efficiency, utilization and access. The individual institution no longer tries to be all things to all patient populations.

Basic, outpatient services have been decentralized, along with specialized services

MANUFACTURING QUALITY SEATING FOR MORE THAN **55** YEARS.

that require short-term or no hospitalization, so patients can obtain treatment in such convenient, intimate and freestanding facilities as neighborhood clinics and surgical centers. Conversely, specialized services requiring hospitalization have been centralized at one or more major medical centers, so that medical specialists, support staff and equipment can be shared by patients throughout the region. Decentralization and specialization have fueled the development of such internal and freestanding services as ambulatory care clinics, birthing centers, children's hospitals, rehabilitation centers, acute and subacute care centers, surgical centers, imaging centers, assisted living, housing for dementia, hospices, and home health and wellness centers.

This division of labor has not necessarily decreased the number of health care facilities, despite the mergers of numerous formerly independent institutions to form major metropolitan or regional medical systems, or eliminated the need for inpatient beds as the nation continues its long-term transition towards greater reliance on ambulatory care. According to the 2001 edition of *Hospital Statistics*™ from the American Hospital Association, there are a total of 5,890 U.S. registered hospitals with 993,866 staffed beds and 4,956 U.S. community hospitals with 829,575 staffed beds. With the United States facing ongoing biological terrorist threats after the attacks on the World Trade Center in New York and the Pentagon in Washington, D.C. on September 11, 2001 and the subsequent anthrax outbreaks in the same metropolitan regions, health care officials may have

to rethink their long-term strategies to account for new and unprecedented demands for services.

Obviously, the best-laid plans cannot prevent the mission of a major medical facility from changing over its 30- to 60-year life span. Just as patient populations continually evolve in size and composition, so do medical science and technology and health care management. Who knows what kind of health insurance coverage will be available to Americans in five or 10 years? This high degree of uncertainty compels the planning of a health care facility to anticipate future reconfiguration, remodeling and possibly expansion along the path set by a master plan which must itself be continually updated. Examples of ways a facility prepares itself include selecting a building site with ample room for further development, designing a structural system to support vertical as well as horizontal additions, and fitting out clinical areas as modular units for rapid conversion.

For all the forces that would tear a health care facility apart and reconstitute it, there is ample opportunity to design a health care environment that offers an inviting, responsive and supporting place for all parties concerned. In part, this is because patients as consumers have more choices, encouraging health care institutions to offer better accommodations as evidence of superior service—and a source of positive, memorable experiences. Another and more reassuring reason is that growing numbers of people, encompassing health care professionals, health care insurers, government, business and the public, are

> *G*racious family lounges, imaginative gift shops, accessible health information centers and cafeterias with appealing decor and palatable food can support visitors and establish officially sanctioned areas where they can convene outside patient rooms.

designed by Odell Assoc., Inc.

MARMOLEUM
naturally

Beautiful.
Durable.
Hygienic.
Cost-Effective.

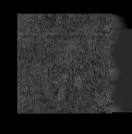

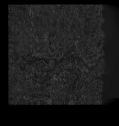

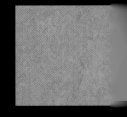

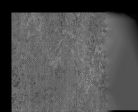

MARMOLEUM® offers a natural solution to all the performance needs that the floor covering of a Health Care facility demands. Plus some more.

MARMOLEUM® offers:

A broad range of colors to match any décor and provide the patient with the most comfortable and uplifting environment possible.

Time-tested durability and reparability, unmatched by any other resilient product.

Naturally occurring anti-microbial properties, proven effective even against MRSA strains, as well as anti-static properties that make cleaning easy.

Simple, low chemical usage, recommended maintenance procedures make Marmoleum the resilient floor with the lowest Cost of Ownership.

forbo
LINOLEUM

convinced that the new healing environments offer superior health care.

Programming: Patients aren't the only people who need better accommodations

Are today's health care facilities being disguised as gracious homes or luxurious hotels? Some of the most recent examples, particularly children's hospitals and senior living facilities, might make the patient wonder. While the resemblance may be superficially striking, health care facilities seem destined to retain key characteristics that will not be found elsewhere.

First, there is no denying the scientific foundation of everything that happens in a health care facility, based on the complexity of medical procedures, the discipline of the physicians, nurses and other health care givers who administer these procedures, and the often intimidating specialized equipment and facilities that support the medical personnel. Then, clean as a private residence or a five-star hotel may be, it does not begin to approach the condition of antisepsis that is mandatory to health care institutions to prevent the spread of disease. Finally, the freedom of choice and personal initiative exercised by the hotel guest cannot be extended to the same degree to the patient.

All the same, today's health care facilities can do considerably more than their predecessors to lower the patient's stress level and make him or her feel more in control of a world that is obviously out of control. Among the ways that are producing positive results are building programs that encourage patients, families, friends and entire communities to become involved in recovery and wellness, space planning that emphasizes wayfinding, minimal distances between related activities and room for anticipated growth, and environmental design that gives patients as much control as possible over the space they occupy as well as visual, acoustic and other sensory links to the world that awaits them.

Patients, families, friends and entire communities can play meaningful roles in promoting therapeutic regimens and long-term wellness, and health care institutions are transforming the mix of activities in their building programs to include them. The objectives are to give patients room to receive families and friends so they can devote their time to visiting rather than staying clear of health care personnel, and to add or upgrade existing areas where visitors can deal with the realities of medical diagnosis, altered household arrangements or the demands of establishing and maintaining well-being.

Wayfinding, the techniques people use to travel from one place to another, can be difficult and stressful in health care environments. Just observe anyone lost in a hospital—due to its size, complexity, revisions, undifferentiated design and contradictory visual cues.

- Patient rooms, for example, have such features as added floor area to accommodate visitors, storage and display space for personal belongings, flowers and gifts, and lounge chairs that open into beds to let family members stay overnight to look after patients.
- On the other hand, gracious family lounges, imaginative gift shops, accessi-

ble health information centers and cafeterias with good decor and palatable food are largely aimed at supporting visitors and establishing officially sanctioned places where they can convene outside patient rooms.

- Reaching out to healthy populations and the community at large also extends the impact of health care institutions in their regions. Young people and families with school age children as well as middle age and elderly adults can be drawn to wellness centers by offering such services as supervised exercise and swimming and nutrition counseling.
- Community rooms can be used to conduct educational programs on popular health topics that acquaint broad segments of the population with sponsoring institutions, and lent to local civic and cultural groups on an as-needed basis.

To be sure, a well-run health care facility must also care for its personnel. Although the physical and emotional needs of doctors, nurses, technicians and other health care providers were often overlooked in the past, they are increasingly being acknowledged with staff lounges and other staff-only facilities. After all, patients are not the only people under stress in health care.

Space planning: Why do people keep getting lost in hospitals?

Space planning can contribute to a patient-focused environment with such

techniques as circulation paths designed for wayfinding, adjacency grouping of related activities, and efficient layouts that use personnel, equipment and data to greatest advantage. While not a rocket science, space planning for health care facilities is complicated by the need to respond and to stay abreast of the changing requirements of service populations, medical science and health care management.

- Wayfinding, the techniques people use to travel from one place to another, can be extremely difficult and stressful in health care environments. Just observe anyone who is lost in a hospital. Fortunately, by consciously addressing the size, complexity, continuous revision, undifferentiated design and often contradictory visual cues of the health care spaces between buildings and within buildings, designers can minimize the confusion by establishing circulation paths with clearly marked corridors, destinations, landmarks and signage, art and other visual communications.
- Grouping related activities around core functions improves internal travel and communications for the medical staff as well as patients and visitors. Shorter distances between destinations mean less travel and confusion, and more person-to-person transactions. Of course, any such groupings are hard to maintain, since the individual components of a health care institution will expand and contract at different rates over time.
- More efficient layouts allow personnel and equipment to serve greater numbers of patients. For example, clustering patient rooms around nurses stations

*M*agical as it sounds, the use of indirect lighting, stimulating colors, textures and patterns, nature and art, and comfortable and attractive furnishings can make an otherwise anonymous and impersonal health care milieu seem far more familiar and assuring.

may enable fewer nurses to maintain visual contact with more patients, alleviating a common shortage in many health care institutions. Putting patient information on-line increases efficiency and accuracy by providing continuously updated facts to everyone involved in patient care, from physicians and nurses to pharmacy and cafeteria workers.

Design development: Restoring a world that illness takes away

The moment you remove your street clothes and slip into a gown in preparation for a physical examination, you sense the loss of autonomy that is part of the price for submitting to a health care facility for treatment. Obviously, architecture and interior design cannot restore the patient's command over the world inside the health care institution. Yet design can increasingly help counter the inevitable feeling of helplessness.

As previously mentioned, a healing environment can incorporate properly planned and equipped spaces for personal belongings, family and friends. It should also afford the patient greater say over his or her surroundings with accessible controls for lighting levels, room temperature, paging, television and privacy, at least within the patient room. Daylight and outdoor views can aid dramatically in restoring the sense of time that windowless and viewless spaces obscure. And the use of indirect lighting, stimulating colors, textures and patterns, nature and art, and comfortable and attractive furnishings can make an otherwise anonymous and impersonal health care milieu seem far more familiar and assuring.

The challenge facing health care professionals and the architects and interior designers who serve them is that much more remains to be done. Patients undergoing scanning in a new, state-of-the-art MRI center are still subject to such stressful feelings as isolation, disorientation and fear, and they are far from alone. However, significant progress has been made, and more is likely as our society continues to close the gap between the original meaning of the word hospital and the reality inside today's health care facilities.

Good design is now doctor's orders.

Roger Yee, an architecture graduate of Yale School of Architecture, has received honors for his work in the field from such organizations as the American Institute of Architects, the American Society of Interior Designers, the International Interior Design Association and the Association of Business Publishers. He has been editor-in-chief of three design publications, Corporate Design & Realty, Unique Homes *and* Contract Design. *In the latter capacity, he created InterPlan, the New York interior design exposition held each autumn since 1994 that is now called NeoCon New York.*

His other activities in the field have included being marketing advisor to Cushman & Wakefield, a national real estate firm, serving as a draftsman and designer to architecture firms, most notably Philip Johnson & John Burgee, and lecturing on design at institutions of higher education, including Dartmouth College and Columbia University. He is currently a contributor to such professional journals as Architecture *and* Engineering News Record, *and a consultant on editorial, public relations and marketing issues to numerous organizations in the design community.*

Alaska Native Medical Center
Design firm: NBBJ

Carpets / Flooring: Bentley, Lees, Johnsonite, Armstrong
Fabrics: Architex, Spinneybeck, DesignTex
Lighting: Linear, Architectural Details
Ceilings: Rulon, Armstrong
Wallcoverings: ISEC, Formica

Anschutz Cancer Pavilion, University of Colorado Health Sciences
Design firm: Perkins & Will

Fabrics: Architex, DesignTex, Steelcase, Maharam, IZIT Leather, ADD, Guilford of maine, ArcCom

Arizona Heart Hospital
Design firm: Stein-Cox Group, Inc.

Furniture: L.U.I., Knoll, David Edwards, Spec
Carpets / Flooring: Interface, Bentley, Dal Tile, Prince Street, Mannington, Armstrong
Fabrics: DesignTex
Wallcoverings: Lan Ark

Baptist Health Ambulatory Care Center, Little Rock, Arkansas
Design firm: HKS Architects

Furniture: Genesis, Peter Pepper Products, Bernhardt, David Edward, Nucraft
Carpets / Flooring: Walker Zanger, Dal-Tile, Pionite, Formica, Nevamar, Prince Street, Interface, Tarkett, All State
Fabrics: ArcCom, Deepa Textiles, Willowtex, One Plus One, Behdheim Architectural Glass, Mannington, Architex
Ceilings: Armstrong, USG
Wallcoverings: Levelor, Koroseal, Crafton, Porter Paint, ICI

Baptist Memorial Hospital - Collierville
Design firm: Earl Swensson Associates

Furniture: Nemschoff, Falcon, Versteel, Thonet, Nevins, Community, Intrex, Hill-Rom
Carpets / Flooring: Interface, Mannington Carpet, Toli Vinyl, Mannington Vinyl
Fabrics: Scalamandre, ArcCom, Carnegie, Unika Vaev, One Plus One
Lighting: Artimide, UltraLights, Lightolier
Ceilings: Armstrong, USG
Wallcoverings: Koroseal, Gilman, Arton

Boca Raton Community Hospital / Cath Laboratory
Design firm: MGE Architects

Furniture: Steelcase, Bradrud, Durcharme
Carpets / Flooring: Interface, Mannington Vinyl, Crossville
Fabrics: Momentum, Steelcase
Ceilings: Armstrong
Wallcoverings: Koroseal

Boca Raton Community Hospital / Emergency Department
Design firm: MGE Architects

Furniture: Steelcase, Brayton, Ducharme
Carpets / Flooring: Interface, Mannington Vinyl, Crossville
Fabrics: DesignTex, Momentum, Steelcase
Ceilings: Armstrong
Wallcoverings: Koroseal

Boca Raton Community Hospital / John W. Henry Mind/Body Center
Design firm: MGE Architects

Furniture: Steelcase, Brayton, Fixtures Dauphin
Carpets / Flooring: Interface, Mannington Vinyl, Dal-Tile
Fabrics: DesignTex, Momentum, Steelcase
Lighting: Scott Lighting
Ceilings: Armstrong
Wallcoverings: JM Lynne, Arton, Koroseal

Bretholtz Center for Patients and Family, Brigham and Women's Hospital
Design firm: Cannon

Furniture: Bernhardt, Geiger, Haworth, HBF
Carpets / Flooring: Bolyu
Fabrics: Scalamandre, Schumacher
Lighting: Zumtobel, LitControl, Boyd, Poulsen
Ceilings: Armstrong

Brigham and Women's Hospital
Design firm: Tsoi/Kobus & Associates, Inc.

Furniture: Brayton, KI, Dutalier, Add, Hill Rom, Neoplitan, Davis, Comforto, Steelcase, Howe
Carpets / Flooring: Bentley, Lotus, Suncraft Mills, Atlas, Monsanto, Dupont, American Olean
Fabrics: Architex, Sina Pearson, Donghia, Arc Com, Carnegie, HBF, Mecho Shade, Deepa
Lighting: Columbia, Zumtobel, Edison Price, Reggiani, Light Solutions East, skytron, Baldinger
Ceilings: Armstrong
Wallcoverings: Tower, Vicretex, Lamark, Schumacher, Benjamin Moore, Polomyx, Formica, U.S. Gypsum

Bristol-Myers Squibb Children's Hospital at Robert Wood Johnson University Hospital
Design firm: Hillier Group

Furniture: KI, Lowenstein, Hill Rom, Corian, American Standard
Carpets / Flooring: Interface, Graniti Fiandre, C/S Group, Armstrong
Fabrics: Maharam, Architex, Pionite, Abet Laminati, Formica, Tana-Tex, Nemschoff Fabric, DesignTex, Forbo
Ceilings: Armstrong
Wallcoverings: Benjamin Moore, Avonite, Walker Products, Forbo

Cancer Treatment Center, Chesapeake General Hospital
Design firm: Paul Finch & Associates

Carpets / Flooring: Mannington Vinyl, Collins & Aikman
Lighting: Leucos, SPI
Ceilings: Armstrong
Wallcoverings: Imperial

Cedars Sinai - Ambulatory Care Center
Design firm: Perkins & Will

Carpets / Flooring: Lees
Fabrics: Avonite, Armstrong, Guilford of Maine
Lighting: Lightolier, Lithonia
Ceilings: Zolatone, Frazee
Wallcoverings: Wolf Gordon

Chandler Hall
Design firm: Klett Organization

Furniture: Akin, Thomasville, Fairfield, American of Martinsville, Southland Furniture
Carpets / Flooring: Durkin Hospitality, Shaw Hospitality
Fabrics: Robert Allen, Valley Forge, Momentum, Samuelson Chatelane
Lighting: Thomas, Corbett
Ceilings: Armstrong
Wallcoverings: Seabrook, Metro, Imperial, Wolf Gordon, Olney, Duron Paint

Childrens Hospital Los Angeles, Marion and John E. Anderson Building
Design firm: Lee, Burkhart, Liu,Inc.

Furniture: KI-ADD, Cramer, Intrex, Fixtures and Furniture, Herman Miller, Harpers/Kimble, Ritter, David Edward, Carnegie, AGI, Pedigo, Softcare, Brayton, Steelcase, Office Specialty
Carpets / Flooring: forbo, Interface, Mannington, American Olean
Fabrics: Arc com, KI, Herman Miller, Carnegie, DesignTex, maharam, Architex, Cramer, Pallas Cares
Lighting: Bega, Nessen
Ceilings: Armstrong
Wallcoverings: Carnegie, American Olean, Marlite, Syndesis, Chromtech, Formica, Koroseal, Wilsonart

Children's Memorial Medical Center / Inpatient Unit Renovations
Design firm: Anderson Mikos Architects

Furniture: Herman Miller for Healthcare, KI-Add, Fixtures, Wieland
Carpets / Flooring: Marley Flooring
Fabrics: DesignTex, Momentum
Lighting: ITRE, Halo, Flos USA
Ceilings: Armstrong
Wallcoverings: Innovations, Benjamin Moore Paints

Christiana Care Health Services Surgi-Center
Design firm: BLM Group

Furniture: The Children's Furniture Co., David Evans
Carpets / Flooring: Armstrong, Interface, Lees
Lighting: Nessen
Ceilings: Armstrong
Wallcoverings: Benjamin Moore, Zolotone, Genon, Innovations, JM Lynne, Carnegie

Christiana Care Health Services Tower Support
Design firm: BLM Group

Furniture: Peter Pepper, Tracey, Adden, AGI, Darran, David Edwards, Gregson, Nessen, Haworth, Seth Thomas, Intrex, ASI, Krueger Int'l, Patrician
Carpets / Flooring: Terrazzo, Designweave, Bentley, Lees, Armstrong, Graniti Fiandre, Dal-Tile
Fabrics: arc Com, Luna, Deepa, Paul Brayton
Lighting: D.M. Lighting, Lightolier, Estiluz, Winona, Shaper, Visa Flos
Ceilings: Armstrong
Wallcoverings: Sherwin Williams, Zolotone, Polomix, Blumenthal, Wolf Gordon, Innovations, Seabrook

Cook County Hospital Replacement Facility
Design firm: CCH Design Group headed by Loebl Schlossman & Hackl

Carpets / Flooring: Mannington, Mipolam, Dimension, J&J Commercial, Harbinger, Bentley, Flotex, Shaw, American Olean
Lighting: Metalux, Lithonia, Rudd, Day-O-Lite, Phoenix, Vista
Wallcoverings: Hirshfield, Korseal, Tower, MDC, Folio, Seabrook, Knoll

Crozer Keystone Medical Office Building
Design firm: Klett Organization

Furniture: Kimball, Highpoint
Carpets / Flooring: Florida Tile, Dal-Tile, Crossville Ceramics, Mannington, Armstrong
Fabrics: Kimball, Guilford
Lighting: Lithonia, Winona, Neoray
Ceilings: Armstrong
Wallcoverings: Tandem, Maharam, Genon, Wolf Gordon, Benjamin Moore Paints

Department of Veteran Affairs Ambulatory Care Center
Design firm: Lee, Burkhart, Liu, Inc. (prime) in association with SMP

Furniture: Milcare, Baker, Midmark, Penco, Pedigo Products
Carpets / Flooring: Interface, Mannington, Dal-Tile, Royal Mesa, American Terrazzo, Armstrong, Pirelli, Mondo Advance
Fabrics: DesignTex, Unika Vaev, Trevira, Carnegie, Knoll, DesignTex, Transit, Prodigy, Maharam
Lighting: Kawneer, Louis Paulsen
Ceilings: USG, Baker Metal Products
Wallcoverings: Dal-Tile, DesignTex

Dr. Bressler's Office
Design firm: Watkins Hamilton Ross Architects, Inc.

Furniture: Homewood Health Care, L&D Upholstery, Ekitta, Keilhauer, Bernhardt, Vecta, Thonet, Cleator, Halcon, Kimball, Nucraft, HBF
Fabrics: Architex, Donghia, Unika Vaev, Deepa
Lighting: Nessen
Wallcoverings: Sina Pearson, Nucraft

Edward Hospital—Expansion for Women's & Children's Center
Design firm: Matthei & Colin Associates

Furniture: Brandrud
Carpets / Flooring: Monterey, Shaw, Amtico
Fabrics: Liz Jordan Hill, Architex
Lighting: Baldinger, Pearce Lighting
Ceilings: Armstrong
Wallcoverings: JM Lynne, D.L. Couch

Fayette Community Hospital
Design firm: Earl Swensson Associates

Furniture: Ekita, Herman Miller, Fixtures Furniture, American of Martinsville, Nemschoff, AGI
Carpets / Flooring: Graniti Fiandre, Prince Street
Fabrics: Fabrication Abba, Maharam, One Plus One, Architex, Glant
Lighting: Robert Abbey, Ultralights, Illuminations
Ceilings: Armstrong
Wallcoverings: Tower, JM Lynne

Georgetown University Medical Center
Design firm: Ballinger

Furniture: Specified Woodworking Corp.
Carpets / Flooring: Forbo
Ceilings: Armstrong

Gottlieb Memorial Hospital - Marjorie G. Weinberg Cancer Care Center
Design firm: Loebl Schlossman & Hackl

Furniture: Kimball, Bright, Bernhardt, Thonet, Allsteel, Knoll, Maharam, AAT
Carpets / Flooring: PermaGrain, Bentley, Shaw
Fabrics: Knoll, Maharam, AAT
Ceilings: USG
Wallcoverings: Innovations, Genon, Vicrtex

Health Central, Ocoee, Florida
Design firm: HKS Architects

Furniture: Brayton, Cartwright, Loewenstein, Tuohy, Intrex
Carpets / Flooring: Collins & Aikman, Dal-Tile, Metropolitan Ceramics, Stafres, Cold Springs, Armstrong
Ceilings: USG

Heartland Medical Center
Design firm: Perkins & Will

Carpets / Flooring: Shaw, Forbo, Tarkett
Lighting: Louis Poulson
Ceilings: Armstrong, USG
Wallcoverings: DesignTex

Hoag Hospital Breast Care and Imaging Center
Design firm: Taylor & Associates Architects

Furniture: Options in Design, ArcCom, Tuohy, Knoll Textiles, John Laurence Furniture Mnfg, HBF Textiles, Walker Zanger, Paul Merril Co.
Carpets / Flooring: Lees, Sisal Tile, DuPont
Lighting: Kurt Versen, Halo
Wallcoverings: MDC, Benjamin Moore

Holland Community Hospital—Ambulatory Care Addition
Design firm: Matthei & Colin Associates

Furniture: AGI, Thonet, Weiland, Herman Miller
Carpets / Flooring: Interface, Prince Street, Bentley, Lees, DalTile
Fabrics: Arc Com, Maharam, DesignTex, Architex
Ceilings: USG
Wallcoverings: Arc Com, Maharam, Lanark, Seabrook

Holy Cross Heart Center
Design firm: MGE Architects

Furniture: HBF, Baker, David Edward, Kimball, Fixtures, Laziboy, National
Carpets / Flooring: Mannington, Lonseal, Constantine, Lees, DalTile
Fabrics: Bretano, DesignTex, HBF, Spinneybeck, Dallas, National, Kimball
Ceilings: Armstrong, Barrisol
Wallcoverings: Innovations, JM Lynne, Koroseal, DesignTex

Hope Children's Hospital, Advocate Christ Medical Center
Design firm: Matthei & Colin Associates

Furniture: Touhy, Gunlocke, Nemschoff, Thonet
Carpets / Flooring: Collins & Aikman, Atlas, Granite Fiandre, Armstrong
Fabrics: Maharam, Architex, Knoll
Lighting: Lightolier
Wallcoverings: JM Lynne, Vescom, MDC, Koroseal

Joe DiMaggio Children's Hospital, Pediatric ICU/Medical Surgical Suites
Design firm: MGE Architects

Furniture: Steelcase, Childrens Furniture Co.
Carpets / Flooring: Marley Sheer Vinyl, Mannington Vinyl, Amtico
Fabrics: DesignTex, Manharam, Steelcase
Ceilings: Armstrong
Wallcoverings: Arton

Johns Hopkins @ White Marsh
Design firm: BLM Group

Furniture: Brayton Int'l, Campbell Contract, Patrician, Martin/Brattrud, Cabot Wrenn, Nemschoff, Jofco, Gunlocke, AGI, Kimball, Children's Furniture Co.
Carpets / Flooring: Mannington, Armstrong, J&J Commercial Carpet, Designweave, Shaw, Bentley, Graniti Fiandre, Carrozza, Mohawk
Fabrics: Architex
Lighting: Nessen, Boyd Lighting, Visa
Ceilings: Armstrong
Wallcoverings: Duron Paint, Polomyx, Zolotone, Lentex, Wolf Gordon, Maharam, Colour & Design

Kaiser San Francisco Medical Center
Design firm: Anshen + Allen

Furniture: Kaiser Manufacturing, Bay Concepts
Carpets / Flooring: Collins & Aikman, Solnhofen
Ceilings: Howard Manufacturing
Wallcoverings: Duraplex

LAC+USC Medical Center Replacement Project
Design firm: Liu, Burkhart, Liu, Inc. in association with HOK

Furniture: Steelcase, Memschoff, Brayton Health Design, Wieland, ICF, Krueger Int'l, Thonet, Howe, Haworth, ADD, Hill-Rom, Community, Kusch, EganVisual, Worden, Conde House, Knoll, Forms and Surfaces, Design Form, DesignLink, Adjustable Steel Products, Nienkamper, Johnson, Falcon, Harter, Davis, Martin Brattrud, West Coast Industries, Gaylord Bros., Bretford, Montel, Gunlocke, Creative Woods, Brandrud
Carpets / Flooring: Karastan, Mohawk, Armstrong, Tate Architectural Products, American Olean, Crossfield Products
Fabrics: Maharam, MechoShade
Lighting: Prudential, Kirlin, Portfolio, Columbia, Ellipitar, Lightolier, Focal Point, LSI, Davis/Miller, Bega, Edison Price, Cooper, Isolite, Basic Source, Staff, Indy, Louis Poulsen, Litecontrol, Shaper, Gardco, Lumiere, Nulite, Advent, Holophane, Alkco
Ceilings: Armstrong
Wallcoverings: Maharam, American Olean

Lemoore Naval Air Station Replacement Hospital and Ambulatory Care Expansion
Design firm: Lee, Burkhart, Liu, Inc.

Furniture: Knoll, Hill-Rom, AGI, Fixtures Furniture, Krueger Int'l, Midmark, ADD, Tuohy, Vecta, Pedigo, Debcor
Carpets / Flooring: Designerwood, Tarkett, Dal-Tile, Mannington, Dupont, Imola Porcelain
Fabrics: Carnegie, Transit, Prodigy, Knoll, DesignTex, Maharam, Mecho Shade, Architex
Lighting: Nessen, Kalwall
Ceilings: Armstrong
Wallcoverings: Dal-Tile, Maharam

The Lied Transplant Center University of Nebraska Health System
Design firm: H.O.K.

Furniture: Martin Brandrud, Maharam
Carpets / Flooring: Collins & Aikman, Shaw, Terrazo
Fabrics: DesignTex, Brentano, Luna, Carnegie, Boris Kroll
Lighting: Gotham Down Lights, American Gold Cathode, Lithonia, Lightolier, Kim, Lumec, Sterner
Ceilings: Armstrong
Wallcoverings: JM Lynne, Innovations, Duraplex, DesignTex

Lilly Clinic
Design firm: BSA Design

Furniture: Bernhardt, Davis
Carpets / Flooring: Armstrong, Bentley
Fabrics: Jack Lenor Larsen Fabric, DesignTex
Lighting: Scott Lighting
Ceilings: Armstrong
Wallcoverings: Zolatone

Lois Pope LIFE Center, University of Miami
Design firm: MGE Architects

Furniture: Acousti, Baker, Hill-Rom, Steris Corp., Fisher Hamilton
Carpets / Flooring: Marley
Fabrics: DesignTex
Lighting: ITRE
Ceilings: Armstrong
Wallcoverings: Innovations

Mary Imogene Bassett Hospital, Ambulatory Clinic
Design firm: Cannon

Carpets / Flooring: Bentley, American Olean, Gatco Coverseas, Innovative
Fabrics: ArcCom
Ceilings: Armstrong, McCarthy Brothers
Wallcoverings: Working Walls, Benjamin Moore, Glidden, Zolatone, Koroseal

Massachusetts General Hospital Northeast Proton Therapy Center
Design firm: Tsoi/Kobus & Associates, Inc.

Ceilings: Armstrong
Wallcoverings: American Olean, U.S. Gypsum

Mayo Clinic Hospital
Design firm: Earl Swensson Associates

Furniture: Weiland, Knoll, KI, Wrightline, Thonet, American Seating, Egan Visual, Hill-Rom, Vecta
Carpets / Flooring: Mannington, Tili, Armstrong Vinyl
Fabrics: DesignTex, Arton, Liz Jordan Hill, Gilford, Maharam
Lighting: Visa, Quoizel, SPI, RSA
Ceilings: Armstrong
Wallcoverings: Tower

Medical Offices of Stratford North, Bloomingdale, IL
Design firm: Anderson Mikos Architects

Lighting: neon by Advertising Products, Inc., custom sconces by NL Corp.
Ceilings: Armstrong, USG

Memorial Care Breast Center at Anaheim Memorial Medical Center
Design firm: Taylor & Associates Architects

Furniture: Gunlocke, Jofco, Options in Design, Pollack & Associates, Arcadia, Suitable Enterprises, Inc., McMurray Stern, Peter Pepper Products
Carpets / Flooring: Lees, DuPont, Mannington
Lighting: Lithonia, Halo, Linear Lighting Corp.
Ceilings: Armstrong, Ceilings Plus
Wallcoverings: ICI Paints

Memorial Hermann Hospital Pavilion
Design firm: Watkins Hamilton Ross Architects, Inc.

Furnishings: McCoy, Inc. Corporate Express
Wallcoverings: Dermacon, Inc.

Memorial Medical Center, Koke Mill Medical Center
Design firm: BSA Design,Interiors

Furniture: Nemschoff, Uptown, Lazyboy, United, Falcon, Herman Miller, Carolina House, DarRan, Milcare, Allsteel, National, Allseating
Carpets / Flooring: Mannington, Armstrong, Lees, Masland, Shaw, Dal-Tile, American Olean
Fabrics: Architex, DesignTex
Ceilings: USG
Wallcoverings: J.M. Lynne, Ianark, Genon, Imperial Wallcoverings, DL Couch, Essex, Koroseal, Victrex, C&A Contract

Memorial Regional Hospital / Joe DiMaggio Children's Hospital Visitors Club
Design firm: MGE Architects

Furniture: Thomasville
Carpets / Flooring: Interface, Mannington Vinyl, Amtico
Fabrics: DesignTex, Manharam
Ceilings: Armstrong
Wallcoverings: JM Lynne, DesignTex

Mercey Cancer Center, an affiliate of U.C. Davis Cancer Network
Design firm: Anshen + Allen

Furniture: Nemschoff
Carpets / Flooring: Prince Street
Fabrics: Maharam, Sina Pearson
Lighting: Nessen
Ceilings: Gordon Interiors
Wallcoverings: Duroplex

Mercey Hospital, Wilkes-Barre
Design firm: BLM Group

Furniture: Touhy, Steelcase, Bonaventure
Carpets / Flooring: Bentley, Collins & Aikman, Designweave, Tarkett, Idaho Quartz, American Olean, Mercer
Fabrics: Fantagraph, Deepa, Carnegie
Lighting: American Glass, Architectural Lighting Systems, Lightolier, Halo
Ceilings: Armstrong
Wallcoverings: Essex, Koroseal, Wallquest, Carnegie, Benjamin Moore, Construction Specialties

Midstate Medical Center
Design firm: Perkins & Will

Furniture: Vecta, Bernhardt, ADD, Kusch, Brandrud, Nemschoff, Haworth, Thos, Moser, People Friendly Places
Carpets / Flooring: Collins & Aikman, Armstrong, Tarkett, Lonseal, Flexco, Johnsonite, American Olean, DalTile
Fabrics: Knoll, Haworth, Carnegie, Unika Vaev, Architex, Pollack & Associates, Cortina, ArcCom, Sina Pearson, Paul Brayton, Custom Design, Halcon, Nucraft
Lighting: Cooper Lighting, Linear Lighting, Flos, ALKO, Nessen
Ceilings: Celotex
Wallcoverings: Levolor, Thermo Veil, Maharam, DesignTex, Pionite, Wilsonart, nevamar, Formica, Abet Laminati, Marlite, Laminart, Benjamin Moore, Innovations, Genon

Morristown Memorial Hospital, Carol G. Simon Cancer Center
Design firm: Watkins Hamilton Ross Architects, Inc.

Furniture: Lowenstein, Fountainhead
Carpet / Flooring: Collins & Aikman, Corian, Thorntree, National Tile and Terrazzo
Fabrics: Nevamar
Ceilings: Armstrong
Wallcoverings: Vicratex Forbo, Benjamin Moore, Koroseal, Glasspan

Mountainside Hospital
Design firm: Hillier Group

Furniture: David Edward, Wieland, Touhy
Carpets / Flooring: Milliken
Fabrics: DesignTex, Brayton
Ceilings: Armstrong
Wallcoverings: Benjamin Moore

NCSF Radiology
Design firm: Anshen + Allen

Furniture: Nemschoff, Steelcase
Carpets / Flooring: Cambridge, Masland
Fabrics: Sina Pearson
Lighting: Prescolite, Artemide
Ceilings: Armstrong, Ventwood
Wallcoverings: Duraplex

New York Hospital Queens, Flushing, NY
Design firm: Swanke Hayden Connell
Architects

Furniture: Steelcase, Brandrud
Carpets / Flooring: Designweave, Shaw
Fabrics: Maharam, ArcCom, DesignTex
Lighting: Midmark, Lightolier, Linear, Alkocu
Ceilings: Armstrong
Wallcoverings: Wolf Gordon, Versa, Koroseal,
JM Lynn, Gilford, MDC, DesignTex

New York Presbyterian Hospital
Design firm: H.O.K. in association with Taylor
Clark Architects

Furniture: Iaccarino & Son

**Northwest Community Healthcare—North
Pavilion**
Design firm: OWP&P

Furniture: AGI, Wieland, Nucraft, Bernhardt,
KI, Geiger, Skyline Design, Children's Furniture
Company
Carpets / Flooring: Collins & Aikman, Bentley,
Permagrain, Caretti
Fabrics: AGI, Arc Com
Lighting: Lithonia, Lightolier, Halo, Nessen
Ceilings: Armstrong
Wallcoverings: Duraplex

Northwestern Memorial Hospital
Design firm: H.O.K.

Furniture: Steelcase, Gianni
Carpets / Flooring: J&J Commercial Carpet
Fabrics: DesignTex, Donghia, Robert Allen
Contract, Brentano, One + One
Ceilings: Armstrong
Wallcoverings: JM Lynne, Parenti and Rafaelli,
Sherwin Williams, American Olean Midwest

NYU Child Study Center
Design firm: Perkins Eastman Architects P.C.

Furniture: Knoll, Steelcase
Carpets / Flooring: Bentley, Dodge-Regupol
Lighting: National Lighting, Wila
Ceilings: USG
Wallcoverings: Benjamin Moore, ICI

**Ontario Cancer Institute Princess Margaret
Hospital**
Design firm: H.O.K.

Carpets / Flooring: Armstrong, Flextile,
Amtico, Fritztile, Interface, Dimension Carpet,
Virtuals, Bigelow, Collins & Aikman
Fabrics: Victor Fabrics
Ceilings: CGC (Canadian Gypsum Company)
Wallcoverings: Vicon

**Palo Alto Medical Foundation / Palo Alto
Facility**
Design firm: RMW architecture + interiors

Furniture: Steelcase, Brandrud, Arcadia,
Woodtech, Berco, Peter Pepper, Fixtures,
Bernhardt, Vecta
Carpets / Flooring: Monterey, Atlas, Collins &
Aikman, Mannington Vinyl, Mannington
Linoleum, Forbo
Fabrics: Maharam, DesignTex, Carnegie,
ArcCom, Luna, Deepa
Lighting: Columbia, Prescolite, Visa
Ceilings: Armstrong, USG
Wallcoverings: DesignTex, Carnegie, Maharam,
Knoll, JM Lynne

The Payne Whitney Clinic Renovation
Design firm: Swanke Hayden Connell
Architects

Furniture: Brayton Health Design, Brayton Intl,
ERG Intl, Gordon Intl, Meridian, Nucraft, Peter
Pepper Products, Steelcase
Carpets / Flooring: Avonite, Azrock, Dal-Tile,
Designweave
Fabrics: ArcCom, Carnegie, DesignTex,
Maharam, Steelcase
Lighting: Day Bright, Lightolier, Tango
Ceilings: Armstrong
Wallcoverings: JM Lynne, Stone Source

**Rainbow Babies and Children's Hospital
Horvitz Tower**
Design firm: NBBJ

Furniture: Design America, Fixtures, Magnus
Oleson, Bonaventure, Bernhardt, HAG, ADD
Carpets / Flooring: Milliken, Interface,
Mannington
Fabrics: Architex, Deepa, Donghia, HBF, Passas,
DesignTex, ArcCom
Lighting: Lightolier, Halo, Tivoli
Ceilings: USG, Rulon
Wallcoverings: Innovations

**Ravenswood Hospital—Community Health
Resource Centers**
Design firm: Matthei & Colin Associates

Furniture: Thonet
Carpets / Flooring: Collins & Aikman, J&J
Commercial, Olympia & Rover
Fabrics: Architex, Maharam
Wallcoverings: Maharam, Vicretex, Koroseal,
Innovations

**Reading Hospital & Medical Center, The
Campus Redevelopment**
Design firm: Ballinger

Furniture: Herman Miller, SMED, KI, Gordon
International
Carpets / Flooring: Shaw, Forbo
Fabrics: Knoll, Maharam
Lighting: Lithonia, Focal Point, Litecontrol,
Delray
Ceilings: USG

Rehabilitation Institute of Chicago
Design firm: Loebl Schlossman & Hackl

Furniture: Hill Rom, Stryker Medical, Kusch, Wieland Furniture, Steelcase
Carpets / Flooring: Interface, Mondo Rubber
Fabrics: ATI Design, Luna Textile
Lighting: Focal Point, SPI Lighting, Visa, Lightolier, Flos USA, Lite Control
Wallcoverings: Wilsonart

Resurrection Medical Center
Design firm: Loebl Schlossman & Hackl

Furniture: Gunlocke, Kimball, Shelby Williams, Intrex, Wilsonart International
Carpets / Flooring: Mannington, Metropolitan Terrazzo, PermaGrain, Durkan, Masland, Bentley, Harbinger, Interface, RCM International
Fabrics: Herman Miller, Donghia, Architex, Bernhardt, Sina Pearson
Lighting: Lightolier, Halo, Alko, Elliptipar, Leviton, Visa, Metalux, Kurt Versen, Appleton, Engineered Lighting Products, Estiluz, Tech Lighting
Ceilings: Howard Products, Armstrong, Hunter Douglas
Wallcoverings: Koroseal, Thybony, Sloan Davis

Samaritan North Health Center, Phase II
Design firm: Earl Swensson Associates

Furniture: Haworth, Nemschoff, AGI, Brown Jordan, Cabot Wrenn, Creative Wood, Fallon
Carpets / Flooring: Lees, Permagrain, Amtico, Mannington Vinyl, Armstrong, Dal-Tile, Ann Sacks Tile
Fabrics: Maharam, Fantagraph, Carnegie, Liz Jordan, ArcCom, Momentum, DesignTex, Stroheim & Roman
Lighting: George Kovaks, Basic Source, Neon, Lightolier
Ceilings: Armstrong, Second Look, USG
Wallcoverings: JM Lynne, Singer, Vicretex, Vin L Fab, DesignTex, Lanark, Essex, Carnegie, Zolatone, Duroplex

Santa Clara Valley Medical Center / New Hospital
Design firm: Anshen + Allen

Furniture: Nieland, Sauder, ICF
Carpets / Flooring: DLW Linoleum
Fabrics: Pallas, Maharam, DesignTex
Lighting: Artup, Elliptipar, Peerless
Ceilings: Armstrong
Wallcoverings: Carnegie

Silver Cross Hospital—Arthur and Vera Smith Pavilion
Design firm: OWP&P Architects

Furniture: Falcon, ADD/KI, Hilrom
Carpets / Flooring: Durcan, Armstrong
Fabrics: DesignTex
Ceilings: USG
Wallcoverings: Duroplex

Somerset Medical Center, Patient Service Center
Design firm: BLM Group

Furniture: AGI, Gregson, Gunlocke, Krueger Int'l, Mity Lite, Patrician, Peter Pepper, Tracey
Carpets / Flooring: Permagrain, Bentley, Interface, Shaw, Mannington
Fabrics: Architex, Momentum, DesignTex
Lighting: Lightolier, Architectural Lighting Systems, Winona Visa, Light Lab, Halo
Ceilings: Armstrong
Wallcoverings: Sherwin Williams, Zolotone, Genon, DesignTex, JM Lynn, Boltawall

Swedish Covenant Hospital / Women's Health Center
Design firm: Anderson Mikos Architects

Furniture: David Edward, Wieland, KI-Add, Brandrud, Sit On It, Lowenstein AGI
Carpets / Flooring: Bigelow, Tajima, Armstrong, Dal-Tile
Fabrics: Sina Pearson, Maharam, Knoll, Paul Brayton, Momentum
Lighting: Boyd, Leucos, Linear, Visa Lighting, Eureka, Halo, Lightolier, Metalux, Square 1
Ceilings: Armstrong
Wallcoverings: Wilsonart Solid surface, Blumenthal, Vescom, J.M. Lynne, Innovations, Thybony, DesignTex, Pratt & Lambert Paints

Swedish Medical Center
Design firm: NBBJ

Furniture: Solid Visions, Office Specialty, Herman Miller
Carpets / Flooring: Interface, Armstrong, DLW Linoleum
Fabrics: DesignTex, Sina Person, HBF
Lighting: Poulsen, Boyd

TMC Advanced Imaging, Palm Valley
Design firm: Stein-Cox Group, Inc.

Furniture: David Edwards, Sit on It, Leland
Carpets / Flooring: Pat Craft, Marley, Armstrong, Dal Tile
Fabrics: DesignTex, Unika Vaev, Architex, Maharam
Lighting: Visa Lighting
Ceilings: Armstrong, Envel
Wallcoverings: Versa, Wolf Gordon

Trexlertown Wellness Center
Design firm: Hillier Group

Carpets / Flooring: Armstrong, Monterey,
Fabrics: Nevamar, Formica
Lighting: Leucos
Ceilings: Armstrong, USG
Wallcoverings: Wilsonart, Benjamin Moore, Forbo, Len-Tex

UCSF Mount Zion Outpatient Center
Design firm: SmithGroup

Furniture: Steelcase, Harper Kimball, Bernhardt
Carpets / Flooring: Collins & Aikman, Mannington
Fabrics: DesignTex, Carnegie, Larsen, Luna
Lighting: Peerless, Lithonia, Finelite, Lite Control
Ceilings: Armstrong, Simplex
Wallcoverings: Wolf Gordon, Decoustics

University of Chicago Hospitals—
Duchossois Center for Advanced Medicine
Design firm: OWP&P Architects

Furniture: Wieland
Carpets / Flooring: Shaw, Caretti
Fabrics: Maharan
Lighting: Elliptipar
Ceilings: USG
Wallcoverings: Benjamin Moore

University of Illinois at Chicago Hospital
Craniofacial Center
Design firm: OWP&P Architects

Carpets / Flooring: Armstrong
Lighting: Columbia
Ceilings: USG
Wallcoverings: Benjamin Moore

Utah Valley Regional Medical Center
Women's and Children's Addition, Provo,
Utah
Design firm: HKS Architects

Carpets / Flooring: Interface, Forbo, Armstrong, Dal-Tile
Ceilings: Armstrong, Cirris
Wallcoverings: Polomyx Paint, Knoll, JM Lynne, Bolta, MDC Wallcovering

Valley Children's Hospital, Madera,
California
Design firm: HKS Architects

Furniture: Bradrud, McHealthcare, Hillrom, Davis, Fixtures, Nemschoff, DFM, Kruger Intl, Versteel, Selby Williams, Steelcase, Pyro Media
Carpets / Flooring: Terrazzo, Tarkett, Dal-Tile, Fiandre Porcelain, Interface, Harbinger, Ti Ping, Dupont
Fabrics: ArcCom, JM Lynne, Gilford, Architex, Momentum, Pallas, Pollack Associates, Maharam, Anzea
Lighting: Artemide, Tivoli
Ceilings: Armstrong, USG

Wayfinding / Virginia Beach General
Hospital
Design firm: Paul Finch & Associates

Carpets / Flooring: Amtico, Collins & Aikman
Ceilings: Armstrong
Wallcoverings: Imperial

Weinberg Community Health Center -
Greater Baltimore Medical Center
Design firm: Loebl Schlossman & Hackl

Furniture: Haworth, spec, GF Office Furniture, Krueger International
Carpets / Flooring: Harbinger, Armstrong
Lighting: Eliptipar, Columbia, Lightolier
Ceilings: Armstrong
Wallcoverings: Zolature, Benjamin Moore

William G. Rohrer Center for HealthFitness
Design firm: Klett Organization

Furniture: Harrison Mitchell, Bernhardt
Carpets / Flooring: Mannington, Mondo Sport, Harbinger, Robbins, Designweave, Dal-Tile, I.C.I., Hubbelite America
Fabrics: Architex
Lighting: Wynona
Ceilings: Armstrong, USG
Wallcoverings: Benjamin Moore Paints, Polomyx, JM Lynne, Victrex, Wolf Gordon

Womack Army Medical Center
Design firm: SmithGroup

Furniture: BT US Army Corps of Engineers,Omaha District
Carpets / Flooring: Senega Tile, Armstrong, Bentley, Johnsonite
Fabrics: Knoll
Lighting: Visa
Ceilings: Armstrong
Wallcoverings: Thybony, Bolta

Woodwinds Health Campus
Design firm: NBBJ

Furniture: Bernhardt, Nemschoff, David Edward, AGI, Old Hickory, Lombard, Versteel, Brayton
Carpets / Flooring: Masland, Lees, Shaw, Interface, Viking Terrazzo, Forbo, Toli, Mannington
Fabrics: Architex, ArcCom, DesignTex, Carnegie, Sina Pearson, Unika Vaev, Paul Braxton
Lighting: Zaneen, George Kovacs, nessen
Ceilings: USG, Dacoustics, Rulon
Wallcoverings: Carnegie, DesignTex, Natural Expressions

W. Stanley Jennings Outpatient Center /
Chesapeak General Hospital
Design firm: Paul Finch & Associates

Furniture: Nemschoff, Falcon, David Edward, Steelcase
Carpets / Flooring: Collins & Aikman, Dal-Tile, Rossi Corp. (stone), Azrock/Mannington, Themec (epoxy)
Fabrics: Maharam, Momentum, Architex, Mayer
Lighting: Belfer, Steris, Lithonia
Ceilings: Armstrong
Wallcoverings: Genon, Exxex, Koroseal

Index by Projects

Let's face it.

Building or renovating a healthcare facility is a major capital investment.

That's why we believe that the leading healthcare organizations of the 21st century will be those that are passionately committed to providing the best possible environments for their patients, staff, and visitors.

Find out how you can:

- Improve the quality of care
- Attract more patients
- Recruit and retain talented staff
- Increase philanthropic, community, and corporate support
- Enhance operational efficiency and productivity

—by using evidence-based design to plan and build your next healthcare facility.

Want more information? Visit our website at **www.healthdesign.org.** You'll find research studies, an extensive booklist, exemplary facilities, product directory, the latest news and information, upcoming educational programs, and much more.

THE CENTER FOR
HEALTH DESIGN

Or, call 925.746.7188 (U.S.) or e-mail admin@healthdesign.org.

The Center for Health Design is a nonprofit, nonmembership 501c(3) organization that serves a network of more than 25,000 professionals worldwide.